2nd Edition

THE EASY MOVIE FAKE BOOK

Melody, Lyrics and Simplified Chords

D1592583

100 Songs in **THE** the Key of C

EASY MOVIE FAKE BOOK

ISBN 978-1-5400-5990-1

HAL•LEONARD®

Visit Hal Leonard Online at
www.halleonard.com

Contact us:
Hal Leonard
7777 West Bluemound Road
Milwaukee, WI 53213
Email: info@halleonard.com

In Europe, contact:
Hal Leonard Europe Limited
42 Wigmore Street
Marylebone, London, W1U 2RN
Email: info@halleonardeurope.com

In Australia, contact:
Hal Leonard Australia Pty. Ltd.
4 Lentara Court
Cheltenham, Victoria, 3192 Australia
Email: info@halleonard.com.au

THE EASY MOVIE FAKE BOOK

CONTENTS

INTRODUCTION

What Is a Fake Book?

A fake book has one-line music notation consisting of melody, lyrics and chord symbols. This lead sheet format is a "musical shorthand" which is an invaluable resource for all musicians—hobbyists to professionals.

Here's how *The Easy Movie Fake Book* differs from most standard fake books:

- All songs are in the key of C.

- Many of the melodies have been simplified.

- Only five basic chord types are used—major, minor, seventh, diminished and augmented.

- The music notation is larger for ease of reading.

In the event that you haven't used chord symbols to create accompaniment, or your experience is limited, a chord speller chart is included at the back of the book to help you get started.

Have fun!

AGAINST ALL ODDS
(Take a Look at Me Now)
from AGAINST ALL ODDS

Words and Music by
PHIL COLLINS

Moderately slow

How can I just let you walk a - way, just let you

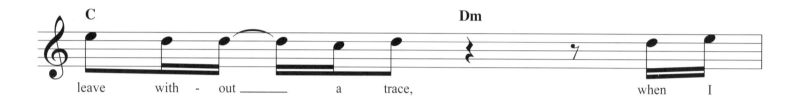

leave with - out _____ a trace, when I

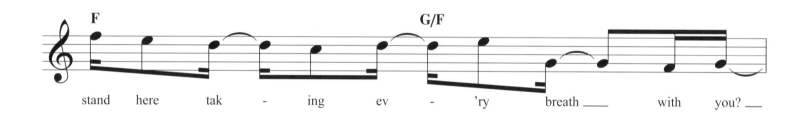

stand here tak - ing ev - 'ry breath ___ with you? ___

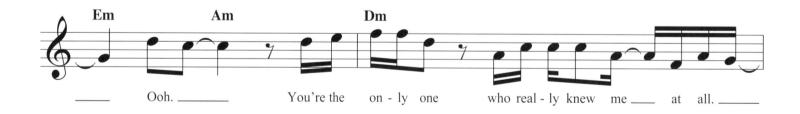

___ Ooh. _____ You're the on - ly one who real - ly knew me ___ at all. _____

_____ How can you just walk a - way from me, when all
wish I could just make you turn a - round,

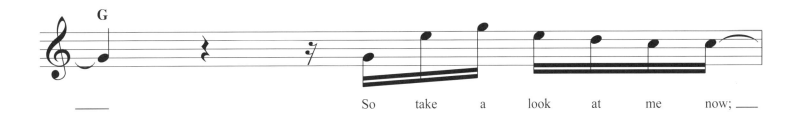

7

emp - ty space. _____ And there's noth - ing

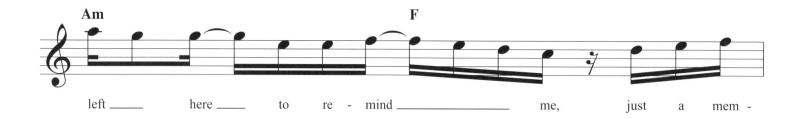

left _____ here _____ to re - mind _____ me, just a mem -

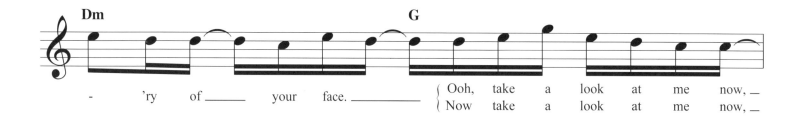

- 'ry of _____ your face. _____ { Ooh, take a look at me now, __
{ Now take a look at me now, __

_____ well, there's just an
_____ 'cause there's just an

emp - ty space. _____ And you com - ing back __
emp - ty space. _____ But to wait __

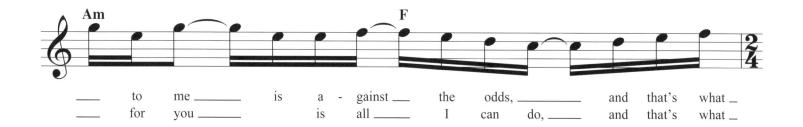

____ to me _____ is a - gainst ___ the odds, _____ and that's what _
____ for you _____ is all _____ I can do, _____ and that's what _

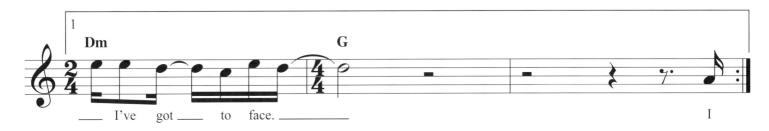

1 Dm   G

___ I've got ___ to face. _____   I

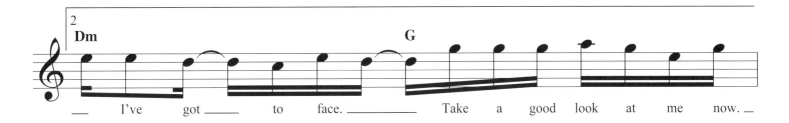

2 Dm   G

___ I've got ___ to face. _____ Take a good look at me now. __

C/G

_____ 'cause I'll _____ still be

D7/G

stand - ing here. _____ And you com - ing back ___

Am   F

___ to me _____ is a - gainst ___ all odds. ___ It's the

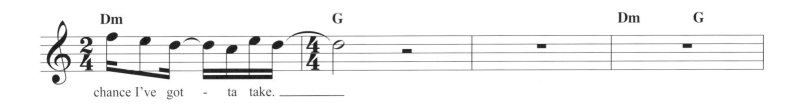

Dm   G   Dm   G

chance I've got - ta take. _____

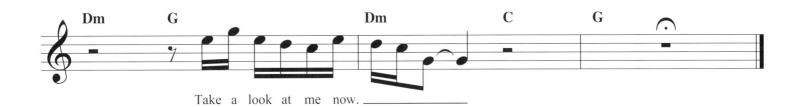

Dm   G   Dm   C   G

Take a look at me now. _____

ALFIE
Theme from the Paramount Picture ALFIE

Words by HAL DAVID
Music by BURT BACHARACH

Very slowly, rubato

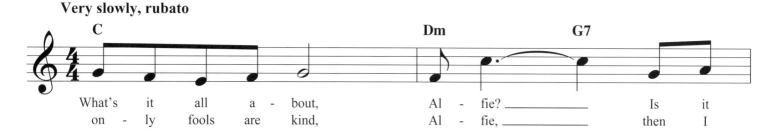

What's it all a - bout, Al - fie? _____ Is it
on - ly fools are kind, Al - fie, _____ then I

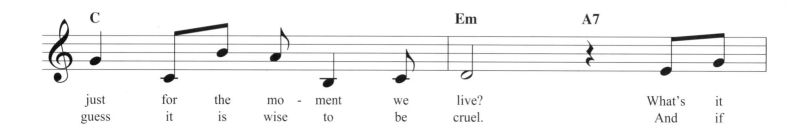

just for the mo - ment we live? What's it
guess it is wise to be cruel. And if

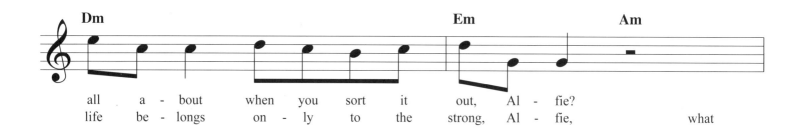

all a - bout when you sort it out, Al - fie?
life be - longs on - ly to the strong, Al - fie, what

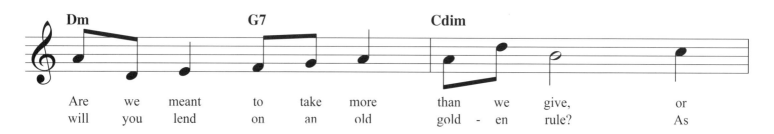

Are we meant to take more than we give, or
will you lend on an old gold - en rule? As

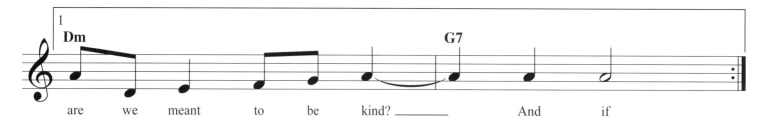

1.
are we meant to be kind? _____ And if

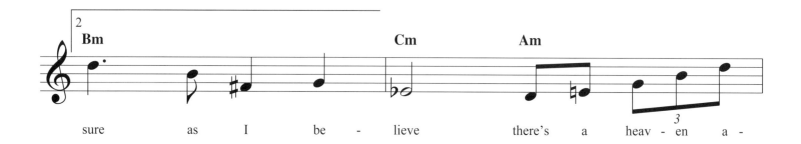

2.
sure as I be - lieve there's a heav - en a -

bove, Al - fie, I know there's some - thing much

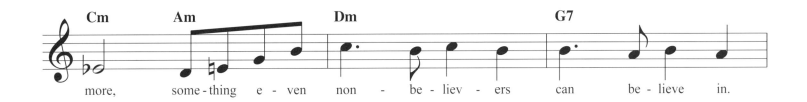

more, some - thing e - ven non - be - liev - ers can be - lieve in.

I be - lieve in love, Al - fie. _____ With - out true love we just ex -

ist, Al - fie. Un - til you find the love you've

missed you're noth - ing, Al - fie. When you walk let your heart

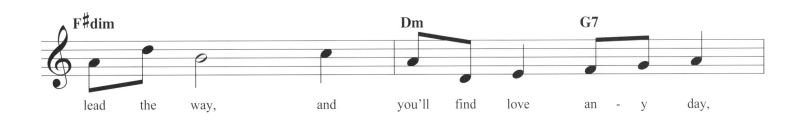

lead the way, and you'll find love an - y day,

Al - fie, Al - fie.

ALMOST PARADISE
Love Theme from the Paramount Motion Picture FOOTLOOSE

Words by DEAN PITCHFORD
Music by ERIC CARMEN

Moderately

I thought that dreams be-longed to oth-er men, 'cause
It seems like per-fect love's so hard to find. I'd

each time I got close; they'd fall a-part a-gain.
al-most giv-en up; you must have read my mind.

I feared my heart would beat in se-cre-cy. I
And all these dreams I saved for a rain-y day, they're

faced the night a-lone. Oh, how could I have known that
fi-n'lly com-in' true. I'll share them all with you, 'cause

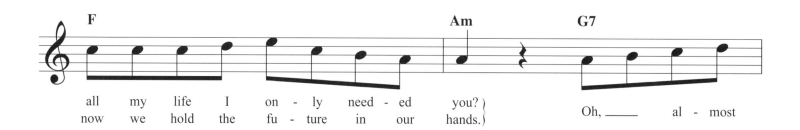

all my life I on-ly need-ed you?
now we hold the fu-ture in our hands.

Oh, _____ al-most

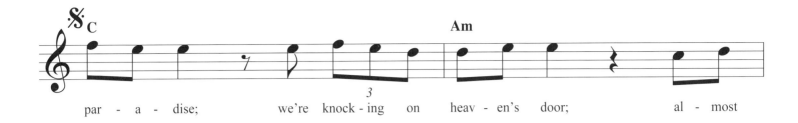

par - a - dise; we're knock - ing on heav - en's door; al - most

par - a - dise; how could we ask for more? I

To Coda

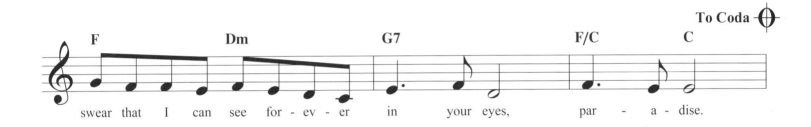

swear that I can see for - ev - er in your eyes, par - a - dise.

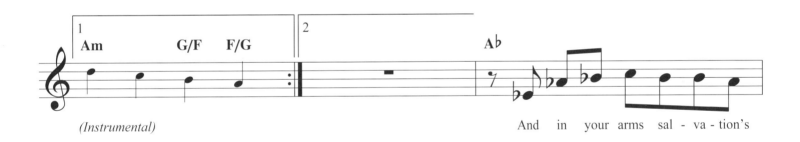

1.
(Instrumental)

2.
And in your arms sal - va - tion's

not so far a - way; it's get - ting clos - er,

D.S. al Coda

CODA

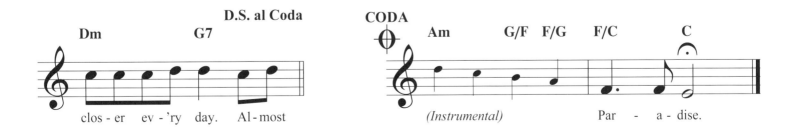

clos - er ev - 'ry day. Al - most

(Instrumental) Par - a - dise.

ALWAYS REMEMBER US THIS WAY
from A STAR IS BORN

Words and Music by STEFANI GERMANOTTA,
HILLARY LINDSEY, NATALIE HEMBY
and LORI McKENNA

Moderate Ballad

1. That Ar - i - zo - na sky
(2.) night, burn - ing in your po - ets tryin' to

eyes. __ You look at me and, babe, I wan - na catch on
write. __ We don't know how to rhyme, but, damn, _ we

fire. It's bur - ied in my soul like Cal - i - for - nia
try. But all I real - ly know: you're where I wan - na

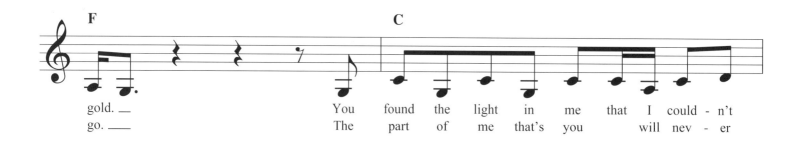

gold. __ You found the light in me that I could - n't
go. __ The part of me that's you will nev - er

find.) So, when I'm all choked up and I can't find the
die.}

words, ev - 'ry time we say good - bye, ba - by, it

hurts. When the sun goes down ____ and the

band won't play, ____ I'll al - ways re - mem - ber us this

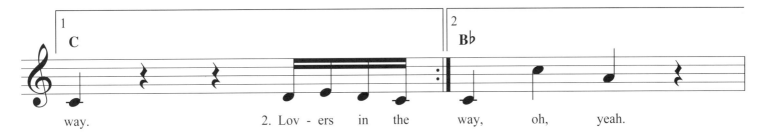

way. 2. Lov - ers in the way, oh, yeah.

I don't wan - na be just a mem - o - ry, ba - by. yeah.

Ooh, ____ ooh, ____ ooh, ooh. Ooh, ____ ooh, ____ ooh, ooh.

Ooh, ____ ooh, ____ ooh, __ ooh, ooh. ____ When I'm

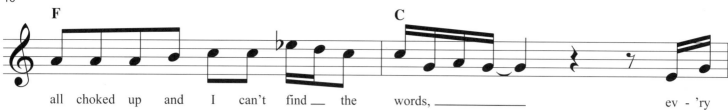

all choked up and I can't find __ the words, _____ ev - 'ry

time we say good - bye, ba - by, it hurts. When the

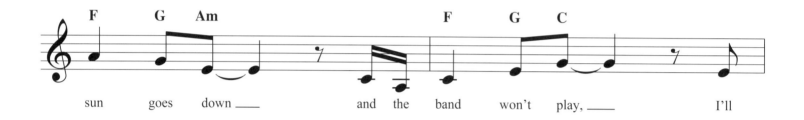

sun goes down __ and the band won't play, __ I'll

al - ways re - mem - ber us this way, __ way, ___ yeah. __ When you

look at me _____ and the whole world fades, __ I'll

Slowly, with freedom

al - ways re - mem - ber us _____ this way. _____

___ Ooh, ooh. _____ Oh, _____ mm.

AMERICA
from the Motion Picture THE JAZZ SINGER

Words and Music by
NEIL DIAMOND

Far, we've been trav - el - ing far, _____

with - out _____ a home _____ but not with - out a star. _____

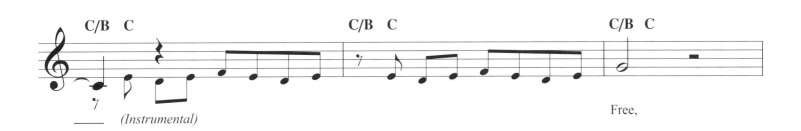

_____ (Instrumental) Free,

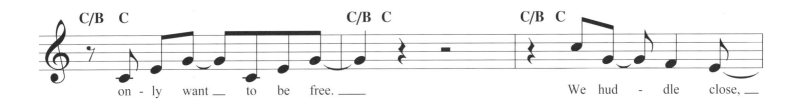

on - ly want _ to be free. _____ We hud - dle close, _____

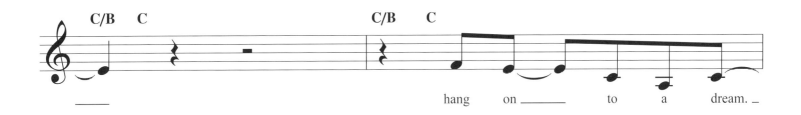

_____ hang on _____ to a dream. _____

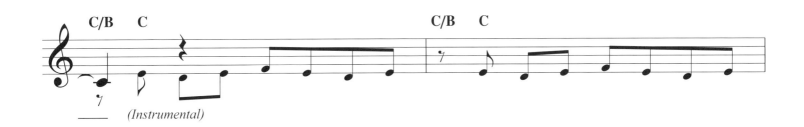

_____ (Instrumental)

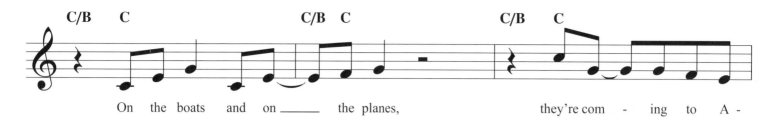

On the boats and on _____ the planes, they're com - ing to A -

mer - i - ca. Nev - er look - ing back _____ a - gain,

they're com - ing to A - mer - i - ca.

Home, don't it seem so far - a - way?

On, we're trav - el - ing light to - day, in the eye of the storm, _____

_____ in the eye of the storm. _____

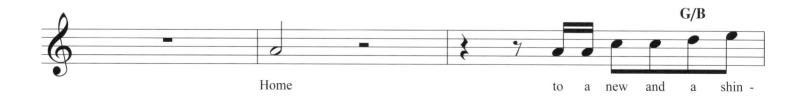

Home to a new and a shin -

y place. Make our bed, and we'll say

our grace. Free-dom's light burn-ing warm,

free-dom's light burn-ing warm.

(*Instrumental*)

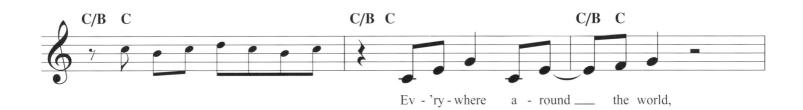

Ev-'ry-where a-round ___ the world,

they're com - ing to A-mer-i-ca. Ev-'ry time ___ that flag's ___

___ un-furled, ___ they're com - ing to A-mer-i-ca.

Got a dream to take _____ them there. They're com - ing to A -

mer - i - ca. Got a dream _ they've come _____ to share.

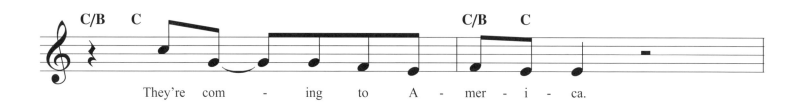

They're com - ing to A - mer - i - ca.

They're com - ing to A - mer - i - ca. They're com - ing to A -

mer - i - ca. They're com - ing to A - mer - i - ca.

They're com - ing to A - mer - i - ca _____ to - day, _____ *(Instrumental)*

to - day, _____ to - day, _

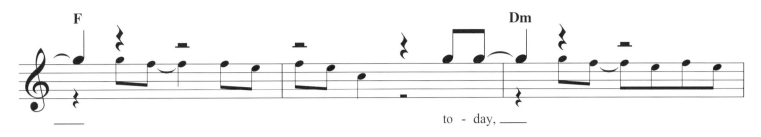

to - day, ___

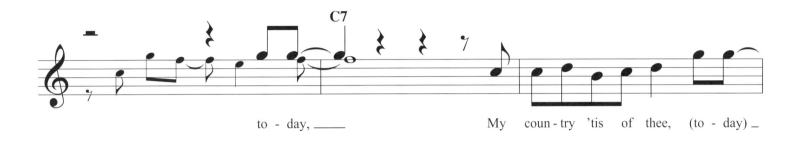

to - day, ___   My coun-try 'tis of thee, (to-day) _

___ sweet _ land   of   lib - er - ty,   (to - day) ___   of   thee   I   sing, _

___   (to - day) ___   of   thee   I   sing ___   to -

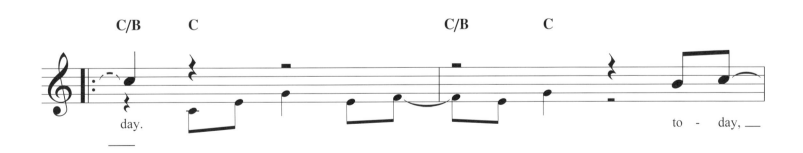

day.   to - day, ___

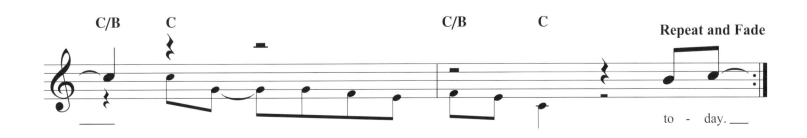

___   to - day. ___

AUDITION
(The Fools Who Dream)
from LA LA LAND

Music by JUSTIN HURWITZ
Lyrics by BENJ PASEK & JUSTIN PAUL

Slowly and freely

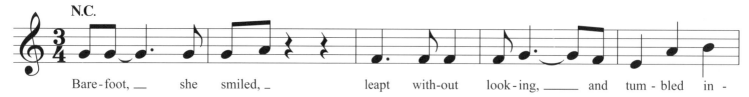

Bare-foot, — she smiled, — leapt with-out look-ing, —— and tum-bled in-

In time (slowly)

to the Seine. The wa-ter was freez-ing; —— she

spent a month sneez-ing, but said she would do it —— a-gain.

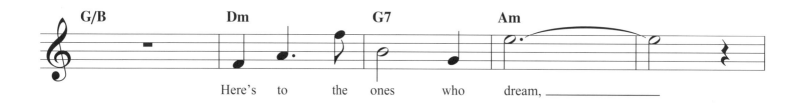

Here's to the ones who dream, ——————

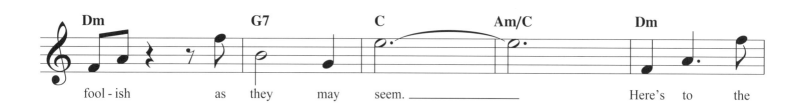

fool-ish as they may seem. —————— Here's to the

hearts that ache; —————— here's to the mess we

make.   She cap-tured a feel - ing: sky with no

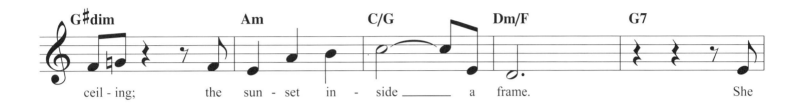

ceil - ing;   the sun - set in - side _____ a frame.   She

lived in her liq - uor,   and died with a flick - er;   I'll al - ways re -

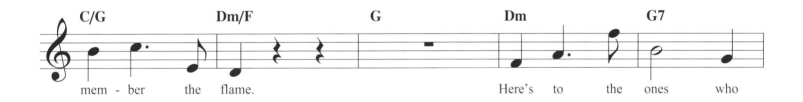

mem - ber the flame.   Here's to the ones who

dream, _____   fool - ish as they may seem. _____

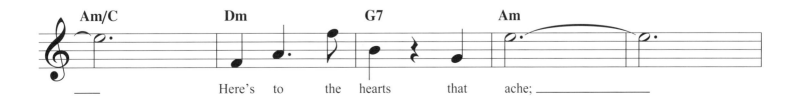

____   Here's to the hearts that ache; _____

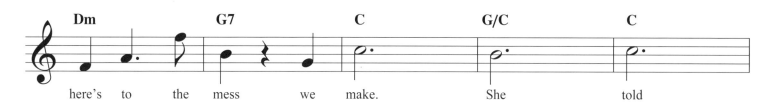

here's to the mess we make. She told

me, a bit of mad - ness is key to

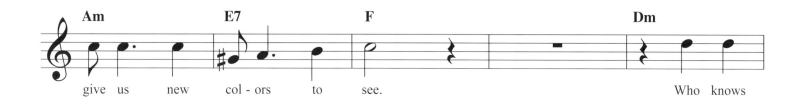

give us new col - ors to see. Who knows

where it will lead us? _____ And that's why they

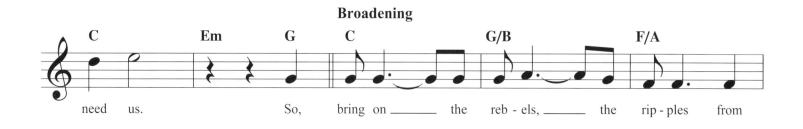

need us. So, bring on _____ the reb - els, _____ the rip - ples from

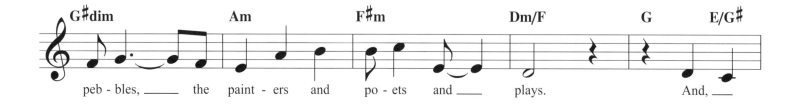

peb - bles, _____ the paint - ers and po - ets and ___ plays. And, ___

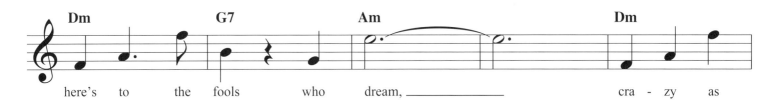

here's   to   the   fools   who   dream, _____   cra - zy   as

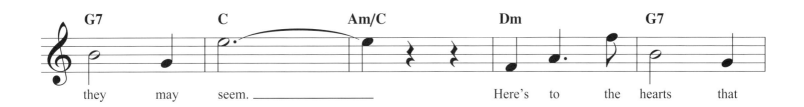

they   may   seem. _____   Here's   to   the   hearts   that

break; _____   here's   to   the   mess   we   make. _____

Slower, with freedom

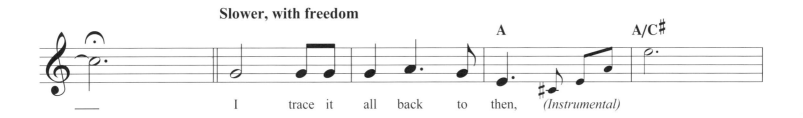

____   I   trace   it   all   back   to   then,   *(Instrumental)*

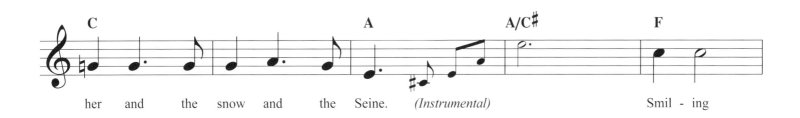

her   and   the   snow   and   the   Seine.   *(Instrumental)*   Smil - ing

through   it,   she   said   she'd   do   it   a - gain.

BABY ELEPHANT WALK
from the Paramount Picture HATARI!

Words by HAL DAVID
Music by HENRY MANCINI

Brightly, with humor

THE BARE NECESSITIES
from THE JUNGLE BOOK

Words and Music by
TERRY GILKYSON

With a lilt

Look for the (1.,3.) bare ne-ces-si-ties, ___ the sim-ple bare ne-
(2.) bare ne-ces-si-ties, ___ the sim-ple bare ne-

ces-si-ties; ___ for-get a-bout your wor-ries and your strife.
ces-si-ties; ___ for-get a-bout your wor-ries and your strife.

I mean the bare ne-ces-si-ties, ___ or Moth-er Na-ture's
I mean the bare ne-ces-si-ties, ___ that's why a bear can

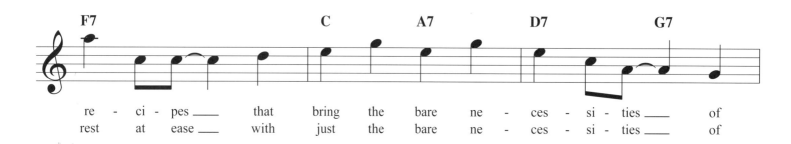

re-ci-pes ___ that bring the bare ne-ces-si-ties ___ of
rest at ease ___ with just the bare ne-ces-si-ties ___ of

life. ___ Wher-ev-er I wan-der, ___ wher-ev-er I
life. ___ When you ___ pick a paw-paw ___ or pric-kl-y
3. So just try to re-lax (Spoken:) Oh yeah! in my back-

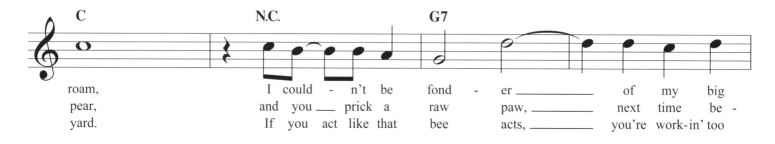

roam, I could-n't be fond-er ___ of my big
pear, and you ___ prick a raw paw, ___ next time be-
yard. If you act like that bee acts, ___ you're work-in' too

BEAUTY AND THE BEAST
from BEAUTY AND THE BEAST

Music by ALAN MENKEN
Lyrics by HOWARD ASHMAN

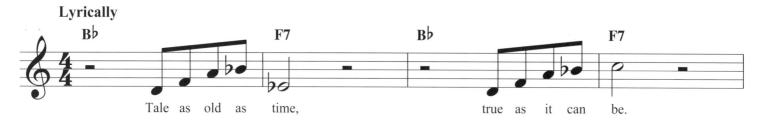

Tale as old as time, true as it can be.

Bare - ly e - ven friends, then some - bod - y bends un - ex - pect - ed - ly.

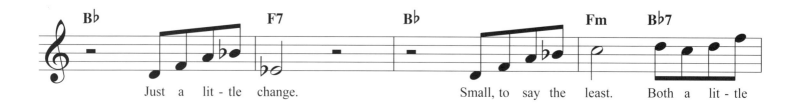

Just a lit - tle change. Small, to say the least. Both a lit - tle

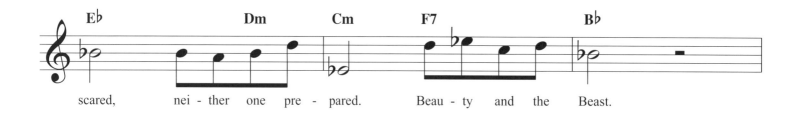

scared, nei - ther one pre - pared. Beau - ty and the Beast.

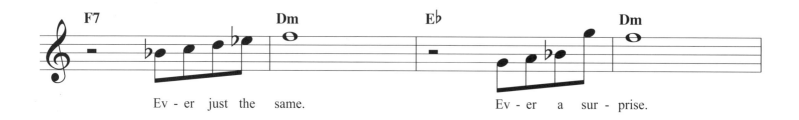

Ev - er just the same. Ev - er a sur - prise.

31

Ev - er as be - fore, ev - er just as sure as the sun will rise.

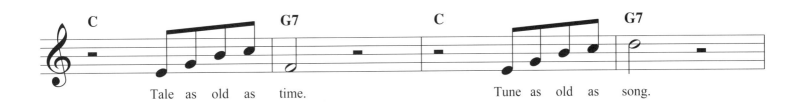

Tale as old as time. Tune as old as song.

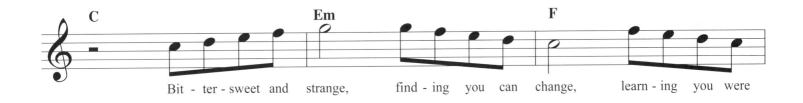

Bit - ter - sweet and strange, find - ing you can change, learn - ing you were

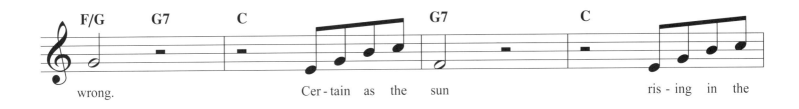

wrong. Cer - tain as the sun ris - ing in the

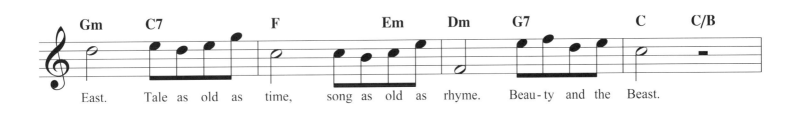

East. Tale as old as time, song as old as rhyme. Beau - ty and the Beast.

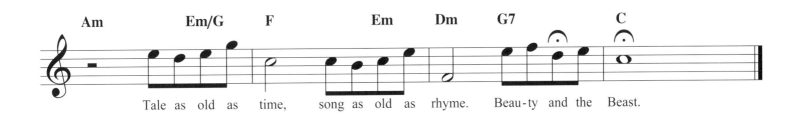

Tale as old as time, song as old as rhyme. Beau - ty and the Beast.

BELIEVE
from Warner Bros. Pictures' THE POLAR EXPRESS

Words and Music by GLEN BALLARD
and ALAN SILVESTRI

lieve in what your heart _ is say-ing, hear the mel - o - dy ___ that's play-ing.

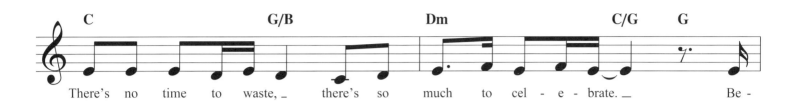

There's no time to waste, _ there's so much to cel - e - brate. ___ Be -

lieve in what you feel ___ in - side ___ and give your dreams the wings ___ to

fly. You have ev - 'ry - thing you ___ need ____ if you just ___

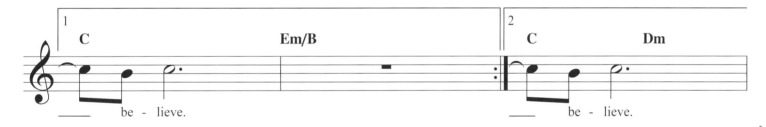

___ be - lieve. ___ be - lieve.

If you just _____ be - lieve, if you just ___

___ be - lieve. If you just _____ be - lieve.

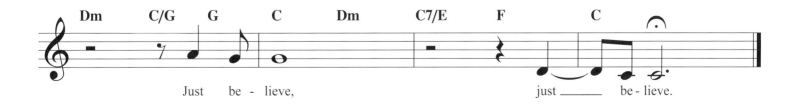

Just be - lieve, just ____ be - lieve.

BIG SPENDER
from SWEET CHARITY

Music by CY COLEMAN
Lyrics by DOROTHY FIELDS

Moderately, with a beat

The min-ute you walked in the joint,

I could see you were a man of dis-tinc-tion, a

real big spend-er, ___ good look-ing, ___ so re-fined. ___ Say,

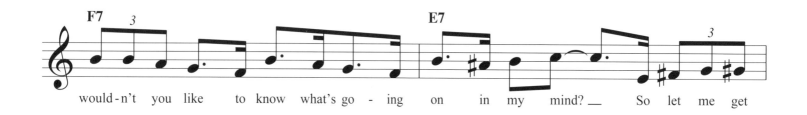

would-n't you like to know what's go-ing on in my mind? ___ So let me get

right to the point, I don't pop my cork for ev-'ry guy I see. ___

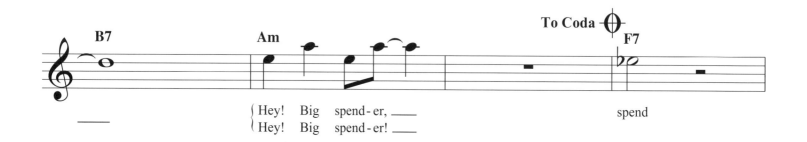

{ Hey! Big spend-er, ___
{ Hey! Big spend-er! ___   spend

a lit - tle time __ with me.

Would-n't you like to have fun, fun, fun? How's a - bout a few

laughs, laughs? I can show you a good time. ____

D.S. al Coda

____ Let me show you a good time. _____ The min - ute you

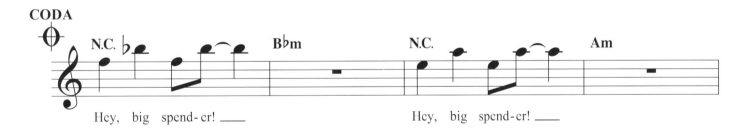

CODA

Hey, big spend - er! ____ Hey, big spend - er! ____

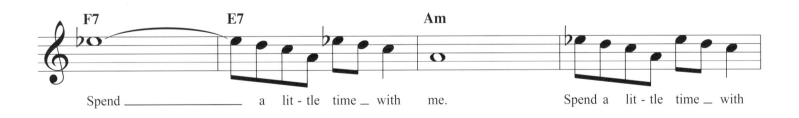

Spend _____ a lit - tle time __ with me. Spend a lit - tle time __ with

me. Spend a lit - tle time __ with me. _____

BORN FREE
from the Columbia Picture's Release BORN FREE

Words by DON BLACK
Music by JOHN BARRY

CAN YOU FEEL THE LOVE TONIGHT
from THE LION KING

Music by ELTON JOHN
Lyrics by TIM RICE

CALL ME IRRESPONSIBLE
from the Paramount Picture PAPA'S DELICATE CONDITION

Words by SAMMY CAHN
Music by JAMES VAN HEUSEN

Moderately

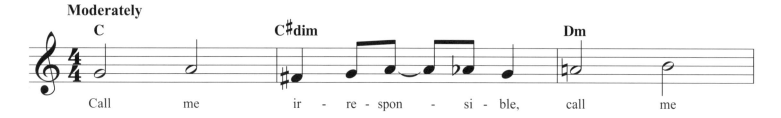

Call me ir - re - spon - si - ble, call me

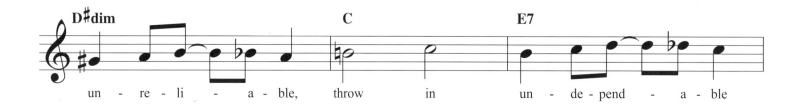

un - re - li - a - ble, throw in un - de - pend - a - ble

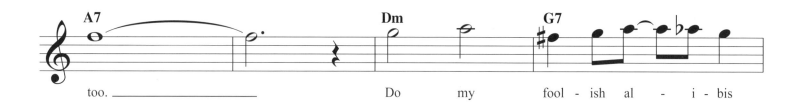

too. _____ Do my fool - ish al - i - bis

bore you? Well, I'm not too clev - er. I

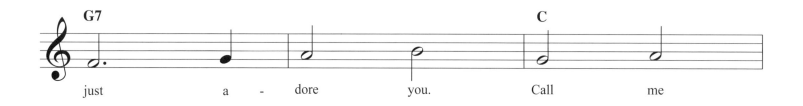

just a - dore you. Call me

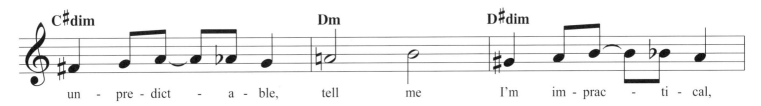

un - pre - dict - a - ble, tell me I'm im - prac - ti - cal,

rain - bows I'm in - clined __ to pur - sue. _____

___ Call me ir - re - spon - si - ble,

yes, I'm un - re - li - a - ble, but it's

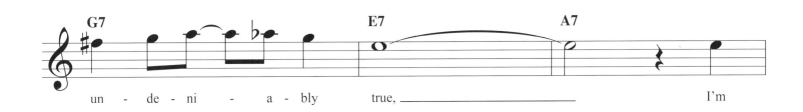

un - de - ni - a - bly true, _____ I'm

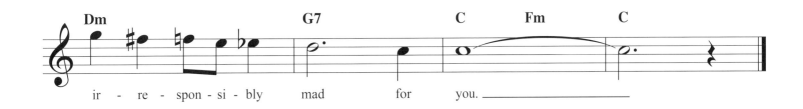

ir - re - spon - si - bly mad for you. _____

THE CANDY MAN
from WILLY WONKA AND THE CHOCOLATE FACTORY

Words and Music by LESLIE BRICUSSE
and ANTHONY NEWLEY

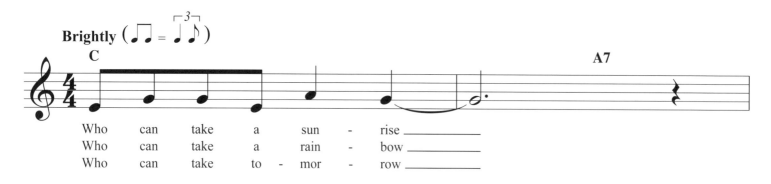

Who can take a sun - rise ____
Who can take a rain - bow ____
Who can take to - mor - row ____

sprin - kle it with dew, ____
wrap it in a sigh, ____
dip it in a dream, ____

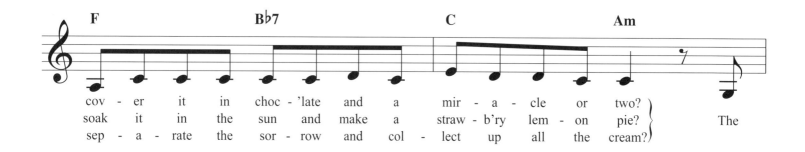

cov - er it in choc - 'late and a mir - a - cle or two?
soak it in the sun and make a straw - b'ry lem - on pie?
sep - a - rate the sor - row and col - lect up all the cream? The

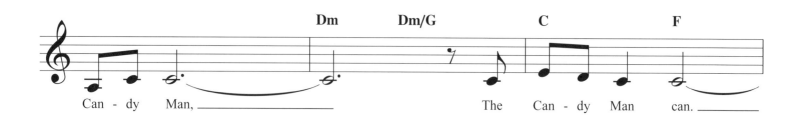

Can - dy Man, ____ The Can - dy Man can. ____

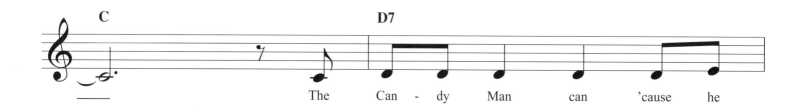

____ The Can - dy Man can 'cause he

41

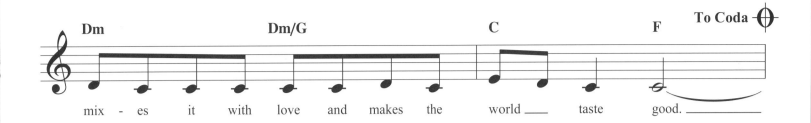

mix - es   it   with love and makes the   world ___ taste   good. _____

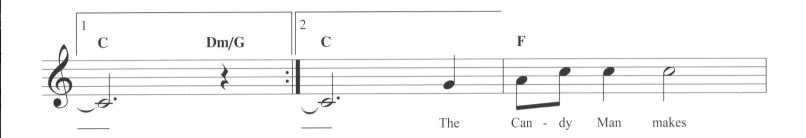

___   ___   The   Can - dy   Man   makes

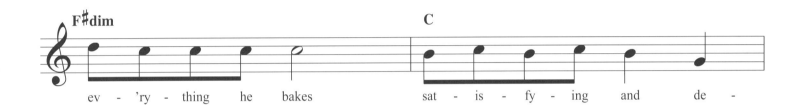

ev - 'ry - thing he   bakes   sat - is - fy - ing   and   de -

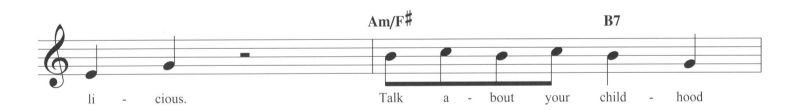

li -   cious.   Talk   a - bout your child - hood

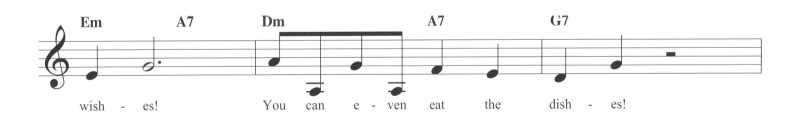

wish - es!   You can e - ven eat   the   dish - es!

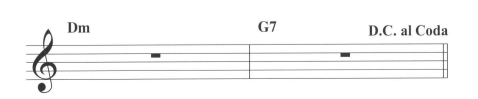

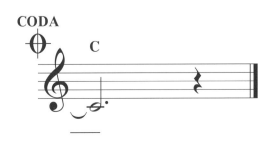

CAN'T HELP FALLING IN LOVE
from the Paramount Picture BLUE HAWAII

Words and Music by GEORGE DAVID WEISS,
HUGO PERETTI and LUIGI CREATORE

CHARIOTS OF FIRE
from the Feature Film CHARIOTS OF FIRE

By VANGELIS

CHEEK TO CHEEK
from the RKO Radio Motion Picture TOP HAT

Words and Music by
IRVING BERLIN

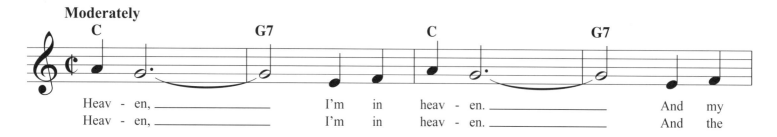

Heav - en, _____ I'm in heav - en. _____ And my
Heav - en, _____ I'm in heav - en. _____ And the

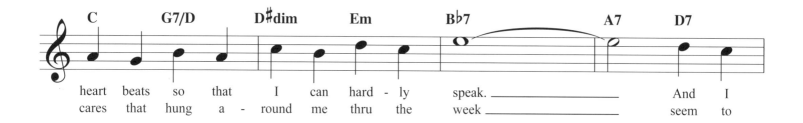

heart beats so that I can hard - ly speak. _____ And I
cares that hung a - round me thru the week _____ seem to

seem to find the hap - pi - ness I seek _____ when we're
van - ish like a gam - bler's luck - y streak _____ when we're

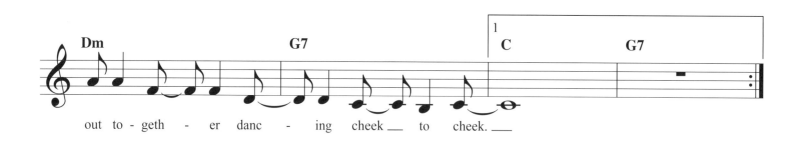

out to - geth - er danc - ing cheek _ to cheek. _

Oh, I love to climb a moun - tain, and to
love to go out fish - ing in a

G7 C G7 C
reach the high-est peak. But it does - n't thrill me half as much as
riv - er or a creek. But I don't en - joy it half as much as
Dm G7 1 C 2 C Cm
danc - ing cheek to cheek. Oh, I
danc - ing cheek to cheek. Dance with me.
3
A♭7 G7
I want my arm a - bout you. The charm a - bout you
G♯dim Am D7 G7 C G7
will car - ry me thru to heav - en. I'm in
C G7 C G7/D D♯dim C/E B♭7
heav - en. And my heart beats so that I can hard - ly speak.
A7 D7 G7 Dm G7 E7 A7
And I seem to find the hap - pi - ness I seek when we're
Dm G7 C
out to - geth - er danc - ing cheek to cheek.

CHIM CHIM CHER-EE
from MARY POPPINS

Words and Music by RICHARD M. SHERMAN
and ROBERT B. SHERMAN

Lightly, with gusto

Chim chim-in-ey, chim chim-in-ey, chim chim cher-ee! A

sweep is as luck-y, as luck-y can be.

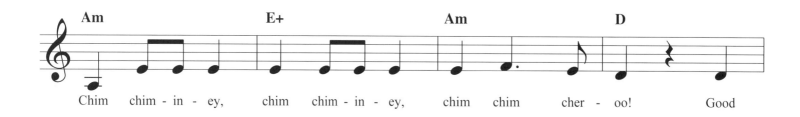

Chim chim-in-ey, chim chim-in-ey, chim chim cher-oo! Good

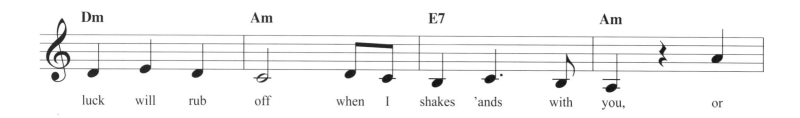

luck will rub off when I shakes 'ands with you, or

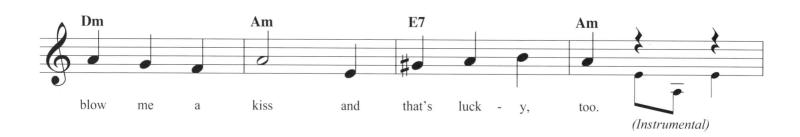

blow me a kiss and that's luck-y, too.

(Instrumental)

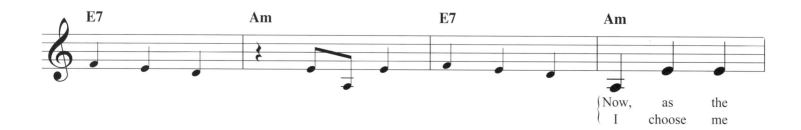

Now, as the
I choose me

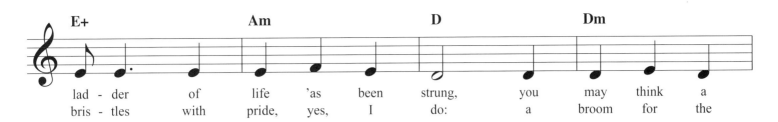

lad - der of life 'as been strung, you may think a
bris - tles with life pride, yes, I do: a broom for the

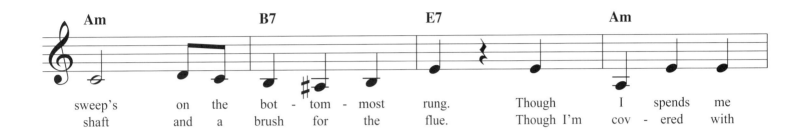

sweep's on the bot - tom - most rung. Though I spends me
shaft and a brush for the flue. Though I'm cov - ered with

time in the ash - es and smoke, in this 'ole wide
soot from me 'ead to me toes, a sweep knows 'e's

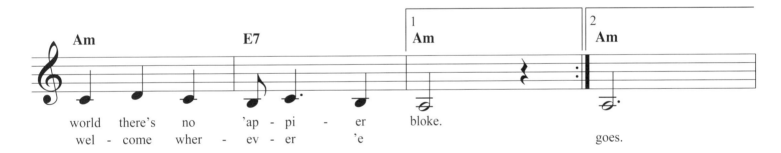

world there's no 'ap - pi - er bloke.
wel - come wher - ev - er 'e goes.

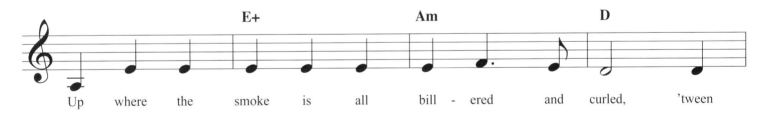

Up where the smoke is all bill - ered and curled, 'tween

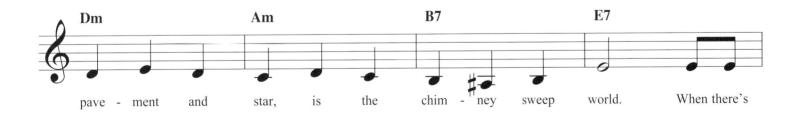

pave - ment and star, is the chim - ney sweep world. When there's

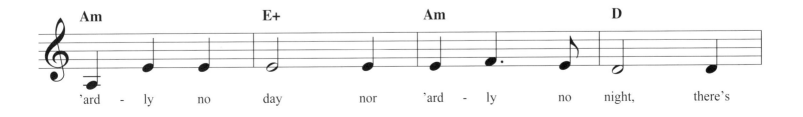

'ard - ly no day nor 'ard - ly no night, there's

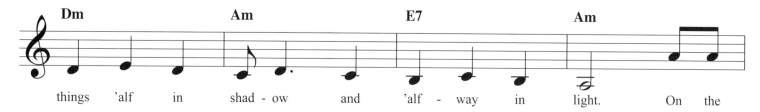

things 'alf in shad - ow and 'alf - way in light. On the

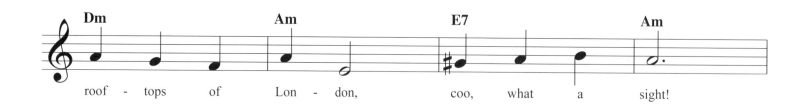

roof - tops of Lon - don, coo, what a sight!

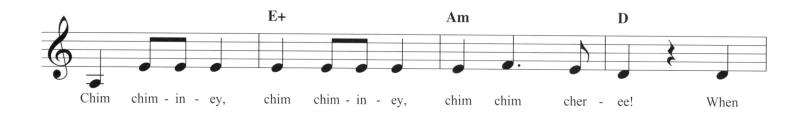

Chim chim - in - ey, chim chim - in - ey, chim chim cher - ee! When

you're with a sweep you're in glad com - pa - ny.

No - where is there a more 'ap - pi - er crew than

them wot sings, "Chim chim cher - ee, chim cher - oo!"

Chim chim - in - ey, chim chim, cher - ee, chim cher - oo!

CINEMA PARADISO

from CINEMA PARADISO

Music by
ENNIO MORRICONE

Simply, with feeling

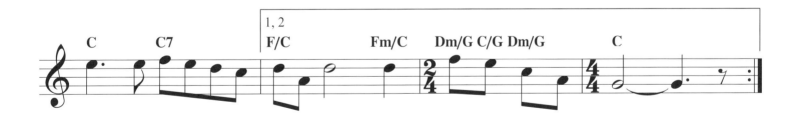

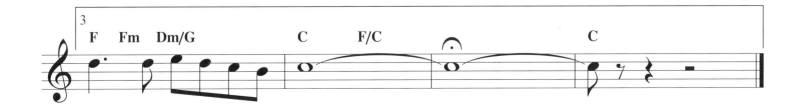

CITY OF STARS
from LA LA LAND

Music by JUSTIN HURWITZ
Lyrics by BENJ PASEK & JUSTIN PAUL

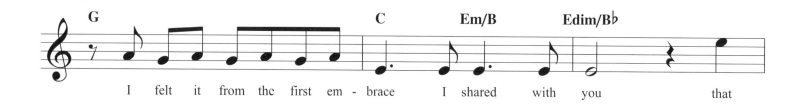

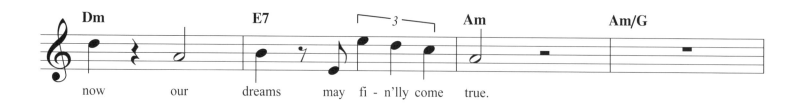

there in the bars ___ and through the smoke-screen of the

crowd - ed res - tau - rants: ___ it's love.

Yes, all we're look - ing for is love from some - one else. ___ A

rush, a glance, a touch, a dance. A look in some-bod - y's eyes _

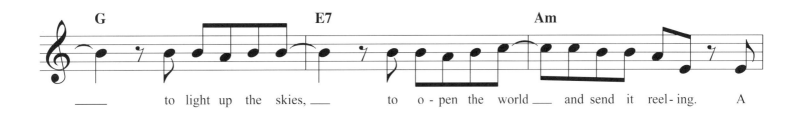

___ to light up the skies, ___ to o - pen the world ___ and send it reel - ing. A

voice that says, "I'll be here, ___ and you'll be al - right." ___

I don't care if I know ___ just where I will go, ___

___ 'cause all that I need's ___ this cra-zy feel-ing, a rat - tat - tat on my heart... ___

___ Think I want it to stay. _____

Cit - y of stars, ___ are you shin - ing just for

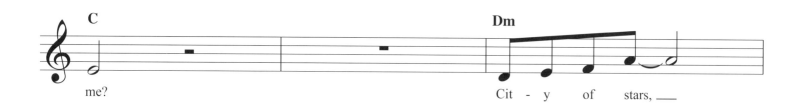

me? Cit - y of stars, ___

Slowly, freely

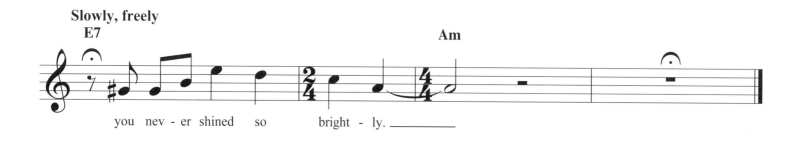

you nev - er shined so bright - ly. _____

DAWN
from PRIDE AND PREJUDICE

By DARIO MARIANELLI

Moderately slow

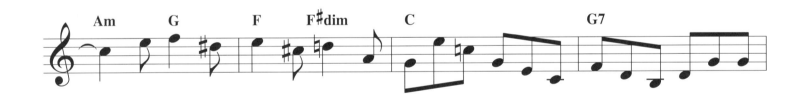

Moderately fast

rit.

54

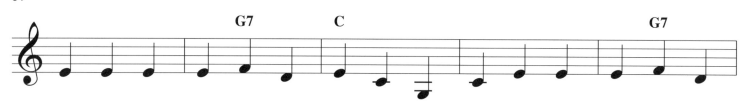

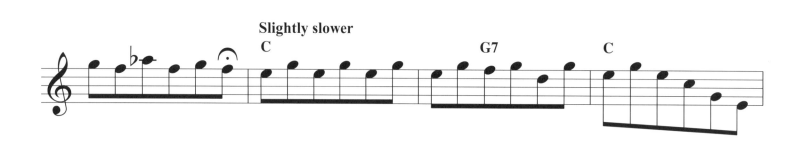

COLORS OF THE WIND
from POCAHONTAS

Music by ALAN MENKEN
Lyrics by STEPHEN SCHWARTZ

Moderately

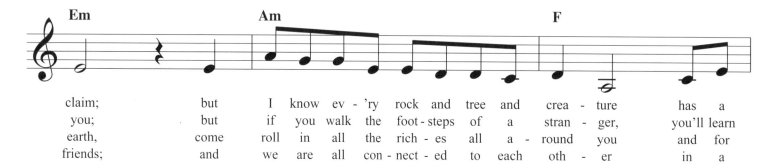

You think you own what-ev - er land you land on; the earth is just a dead thing you can
think the on - ly peo - ple who are peo - ple are the peo - ple who look and think like
run the hid - den pine trails of the for - est, come taste the sun-sweet ber - ries of the
rain-storm and the riv - er are my broth-ers; the her-on and the ot - ter are my

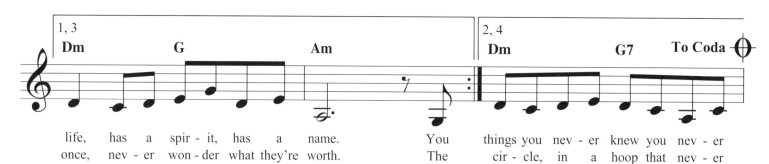

claim; but I know ev - 'ry rock and tree and crea - ture has a
you; but if you walk the foot-steps of a stran - ger, you'll learn
earth, come roll in all the rich - es all a - round you and for
friends; and we are all con-nect-ed to each oth - er in a

life, has a spir - it, has a name. You
once, nev - er won - der what they're worth. The

things you nev - er knew you nev - er
cir - cle, in a hoop that nev - er

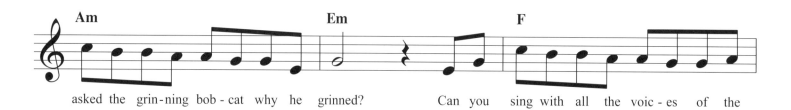

knew. Have you ev - er heard the wolf cry to the blue corn moon or

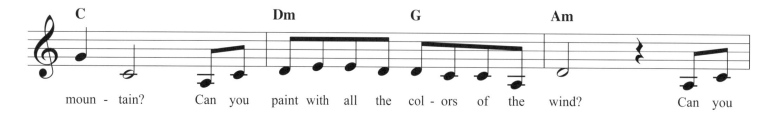

asked the grin-ning bob - cat why he grinned? Can you sing with all the voic - es of the

moun - tain? Can you paint with all the col - ors of the wind? Can you

D.S. al Coda (take repeat)

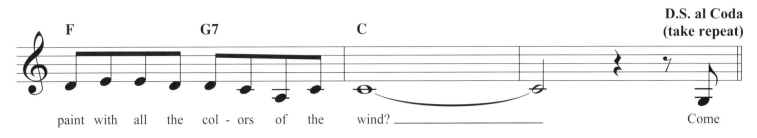

paint with all the col - ors of the wind? _____ Come

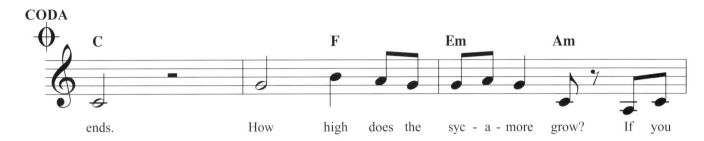

CODA

ends. How high does the syc - a - more grow? If you

cut it down then you'll nev - er know. And you'll

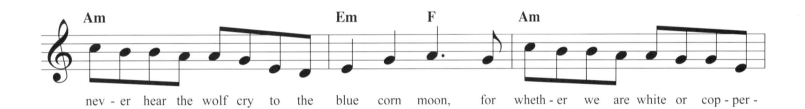

nev - er hear the wolf cry to the blue corn moon, for wheth - er we are white or cop - per -

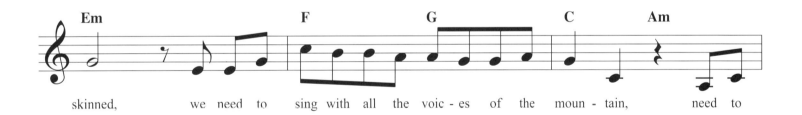

skinned, we need to sing with all the voic - es of the moun - tain, need to

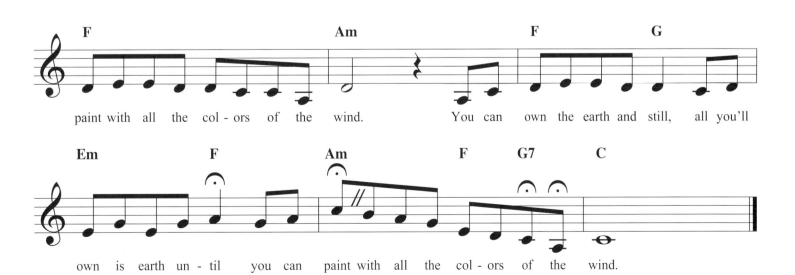

paint with all the col - ors of the wind. You can own the earth and still, all you'll

own is earth un - til you can paint with all the col - ors of the wind.

COME WHAT MAY
from the Motion Picture MOULIN ROUGE

Words and Music by DAVID BAERWALD
and KEVIN GILBERT

Slowly

Male: Nev-er knew I could feel _____ like this, ___

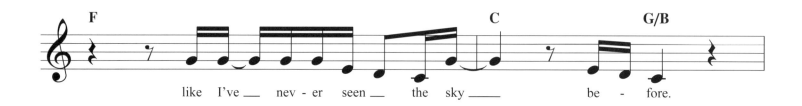

like I've ___ nev-er seen ___ the sky _____ be - fore.

Want to van - ish in - side _____ your kiss. ___

Ev - 'ry day ___ I love ___ you more and ___ more.

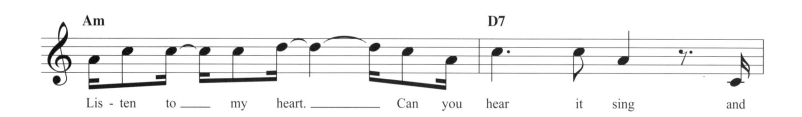

Lis - ten to _____ my heart. _____ Can you hear it sing and

tell - ing me ___ to give _____ you ev - 'ry - thing?

Sea - sons _____ may change, _____ win - ter to spring,

but I love you un - til the end of

time. Come what may, _____ come what may, _____

_____ I will love you un - til my dy - ing _____

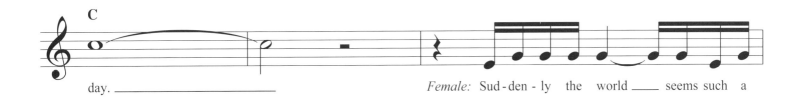

day. _____ *Female:* Sud - den - ly the world _____ seems such a

per - fect place. Sud - den - ly it moves with such _____ a

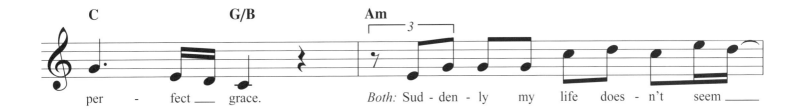

per - fect _____ grace. *Both:* Sud - den - ly my life does - n't seem _____

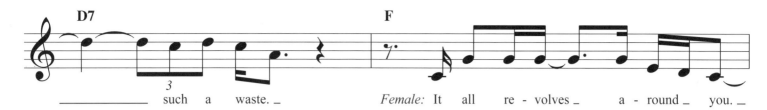

such a waste. _ *Female:* It all re - volves _ a - round _ you. _

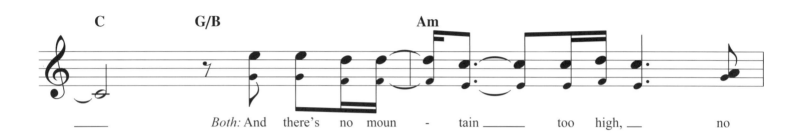

_ *Both:* And there's no moun - tain _ too high, _ no

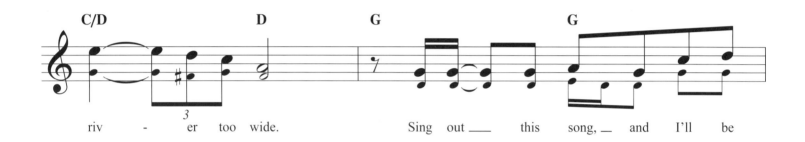

riv - er too wide. Sing out _ this song, _ and I'll be

there _ by your side. _ _ Storm clouds may gath - er and stars _ may col-lide,

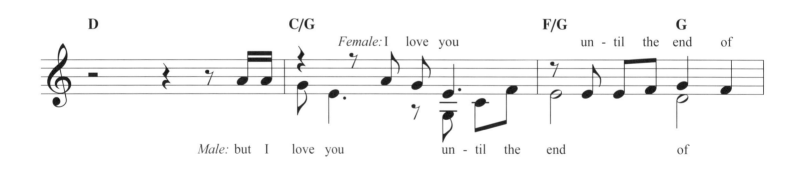

Female: I love you un - til the end of

Male: but I love you un - til the end of

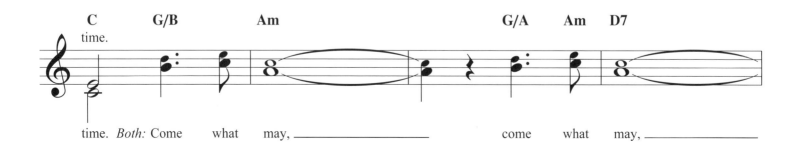

time.

time. *Both:* Come what may, _____ come what may, _____

61

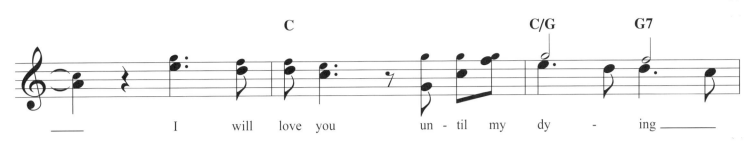

I will love you un - til my dy - ing _____

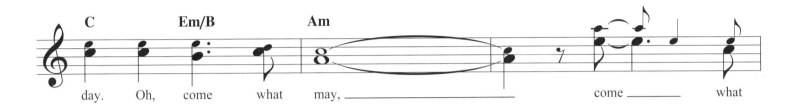

day. Oh, come what may, _____ come _____ what

may _____ I will love, _____ I will love you.

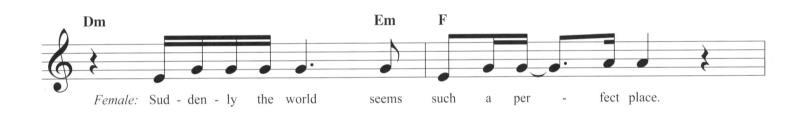

Female: Sud - den - ly the world seems such a per - fect place.

Both: Come what may, come what

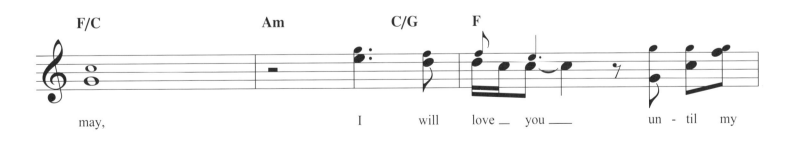

may, I will love _ you _ un - til my

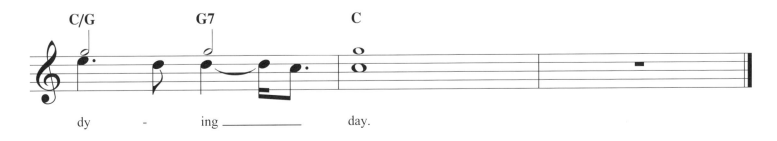

dy - ing _____ day.

DIAMONDS ARE A GIRL'S BEST FRIEND
from GENTLEMEN PREFER BLONDES

Words by LEO ROBIN
Music by JULE STYNE

A kiss on the hand may be quite con - ti - nen - tal but
may come a time when a lass needs a law - yer, but

dia - monds are a girl's best friend. _____ A kiss may be grand but it
dia - monds are a girl's best friend. _____ There may come a time when a

won't pay the ren - tal on your hum - ble flat _____ or help you at the au - to - mat.
hard - boiled em - ploy - er thinks you're aw - ful nice, _____ but get that "ice" or else no dice.

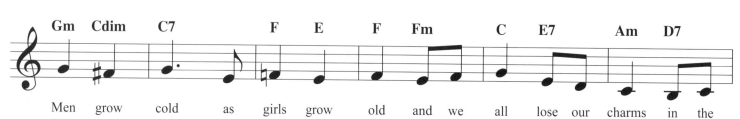

Men grow cold as girls grow old and we all lose our charms in the
He's your guy when stocks are high, but be - ware when they start to de -

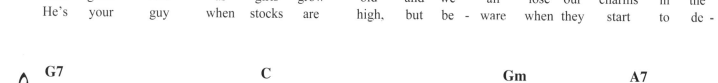

end. _____ But square - cut or pear - shape these rocks don't lose their shape,
scend. _____ It's then that those lous - es go back to their spous - es,

dia - monds are a girl's best friend. _____ There
dia - monds are a girl's best friend. _____

DON'T CRY FOR ME ARGENTINA
from EVITA

Words by TIM RICE
Music by ANDREW LLOYD WEBBER

Slowly

It won't be eas-y. You'll think it

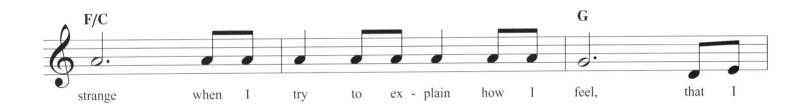

strange when I try to ex-plain how I feel, that I

still need your love af-ter all that I've done. You won't be-

lieve me. All you will see is a girl you once knew al-

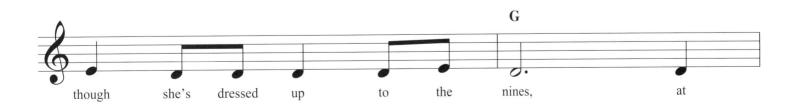

though she's dressed up to the nines, at

64

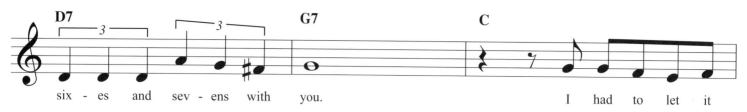

six - es and sev - ens with you. I had to let it

hap - pen, I had to change. Could - n't stay all my life down at

heel look - ing out of the win - dow, stay - ing out of the sun.

So I chose free - dom, run - ning a - round try - ing

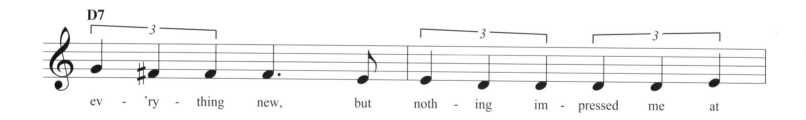

ev - 'ry - thing new, but noth - ing im - pressed me at

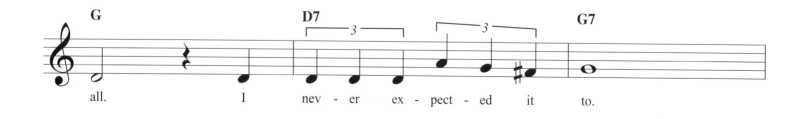

all. I nev - er ex - pect - ed it to.

Don't cry for me Ar - gen - tin - a. The

truth is I nev - er left you. All through my wild days, ___ my mad ex -

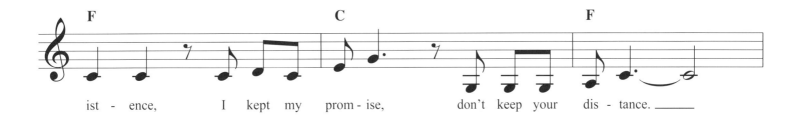

ist - ence, I kept my prom - ise, don't keep your dis - tance. _____

Have I said too much? There's noth - ing more I can think of to

say to you. But all you have to do is

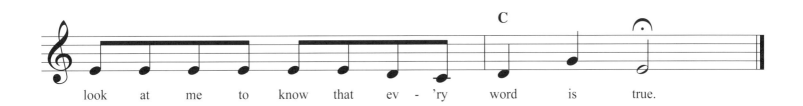

look at me to know that ev - 'ry word is true.

ENDLESS LOVE
from ENDLESS LOVE

Words and Music by
LIONEL RICHIE

EVERYBODY'S TALKIN'
(Echoes)
from MIDNIGHT COWBOY

Words and Music by
FRED NEIL

Moderately

Ev - 'ry - bod - y's   talk - in' at me.   I don't hear a

word they're say - in',   on - ly the ech - oes _____ of my

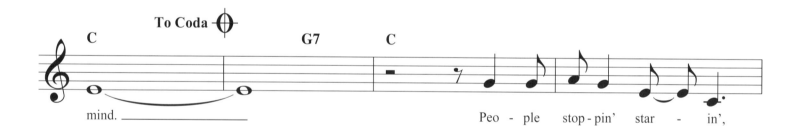

mind. _____   Peo - ple stop - pin' star - in',

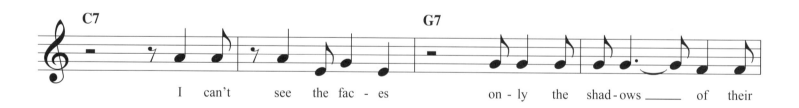

I can't   see the fac - es   on - ly the shad - ows _____ of their

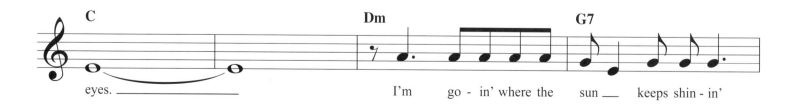

eyes. _____   I'm   go - in' where the sun ___ keeps shin - in'

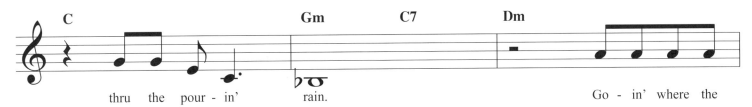

thru the pour - in' rain. Go - in' where the

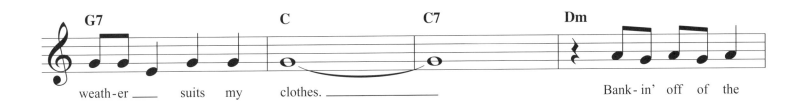

weath-er ____ suits my clothes. _____ Bank-in' off of the

north - east wind. Sail - in' on a sum - mer breeze.

D.C. al Coda

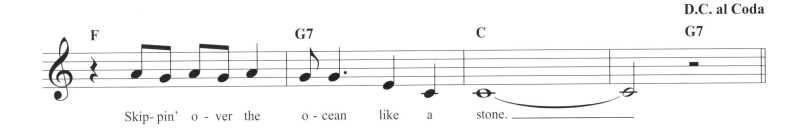

Skip-pin' o - ver the o - cean like a stone. _____

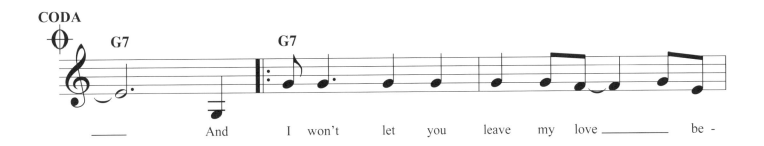

____ And I won't let you leave my love ____ be -

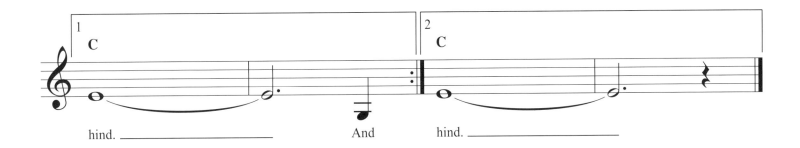

hind. _____ And hind. _____

(Everything I Do)

I DO IT FOR YOU

from the Motion Picture ROBIN HOOD: PRINCE OF THIEVES

Words and Music by BRYAN ADAMS,
R.J. LANGE and MICHAEL KAMEN

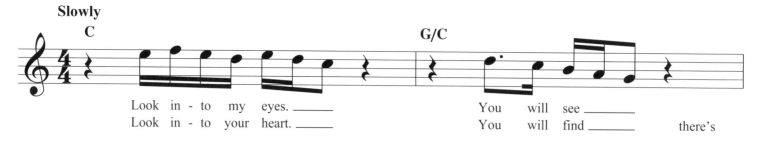

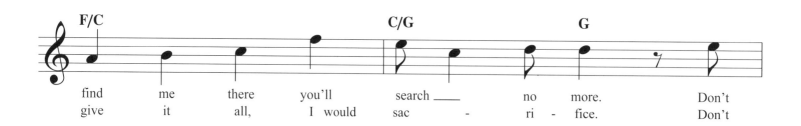

71

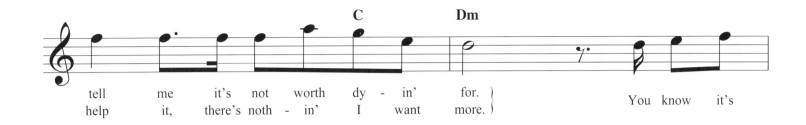

tell me it's not worth dy - in' for.
help it, there's noth - in' I want more.

You know it's

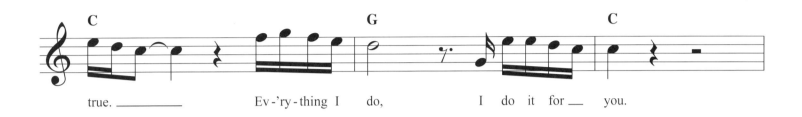

true. _____ Ev-'ry-thing I do, I do it for __ you.

There's no love like your love and no

oth - er could give more __ love, there's no - where _____ un - less

you're there all the time, _____ all the way __ yeah. _____

__ *(Instrumental)*

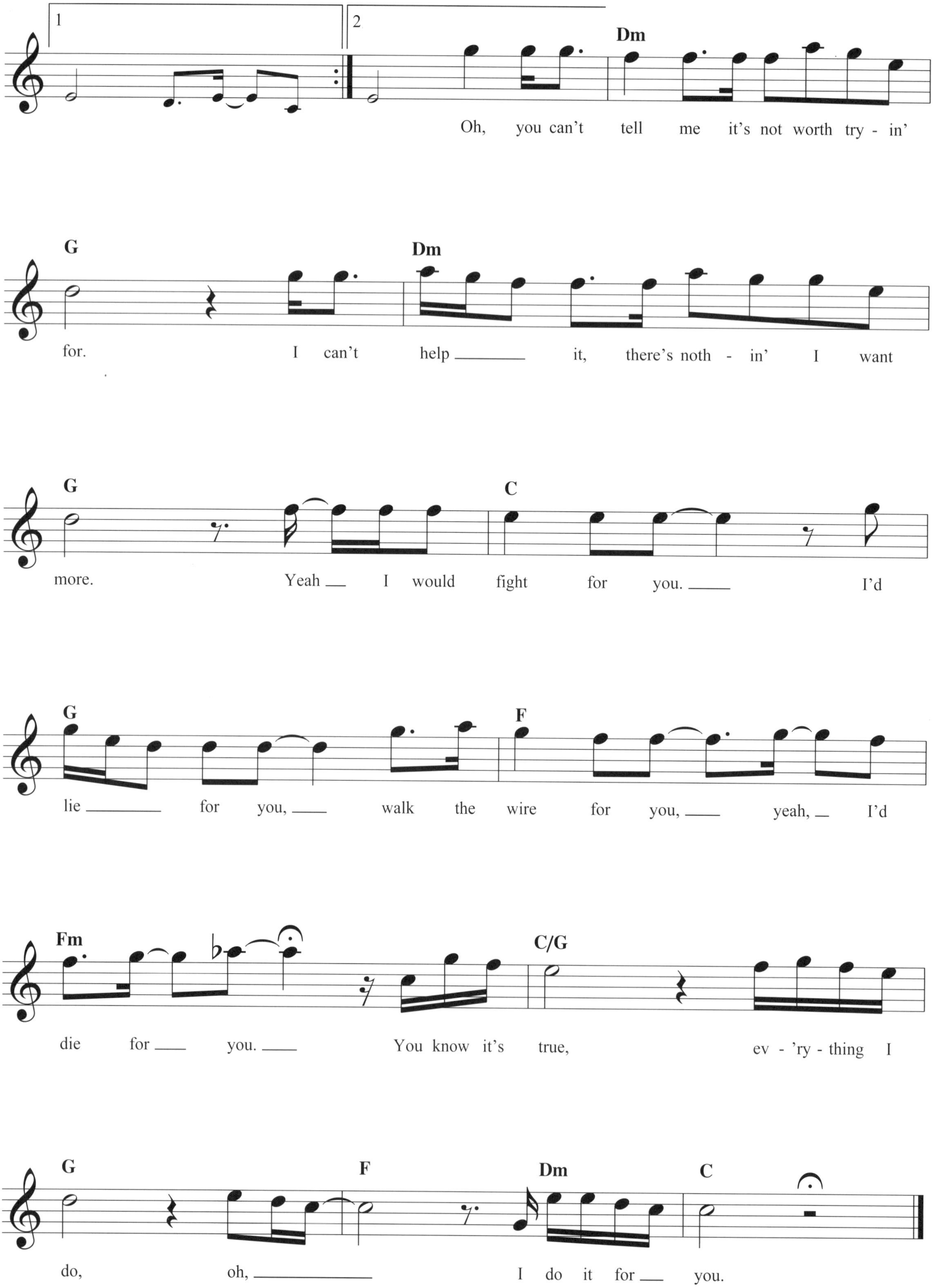
1
2
Dm
Oh, you can't tell me it's not worth try - in'
G
Dm
for. I can't help it, there's noth - in' I want
G
C
more. Yeah I would fight for you. I'd
G
F
lie for you, walk the wire for you, yeah, I'd
Fm
C/G
die for you. You know it's true, ev - 'ry - thing I
G
F
Dm
C
do, oh, I do it for you.

FLASHDANCE...WHAT A FEELING
from the Paramount Picture FLASHDANCE

Words by KEITH FORSEY and IRENE CARA
Music by GIORGIO MORODER

Steadily

First, when there's noth-ing but a slow glow-ing

dream, _____ that your fear seems to hide deep in-

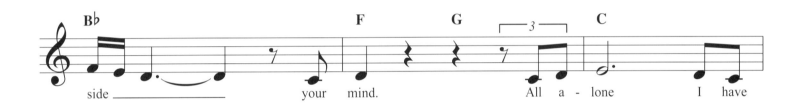

side _____ your mind. All a-lone I have

cried si-lent tears full of pride _____ in a

Faster, with a driving beat

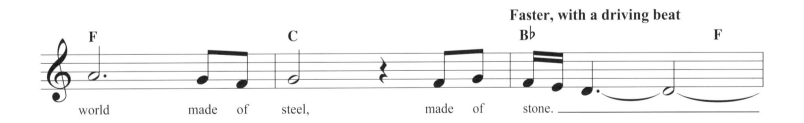

world made of steel, made of stone. _____

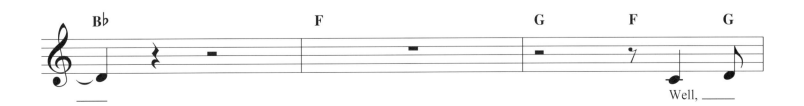

_____ Well, _____

74

75

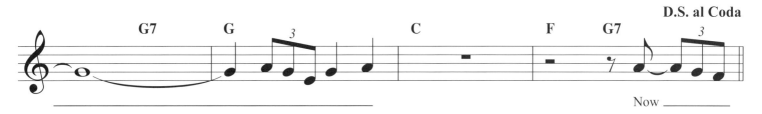

Now _____

CODA

What a feel - ing. _____

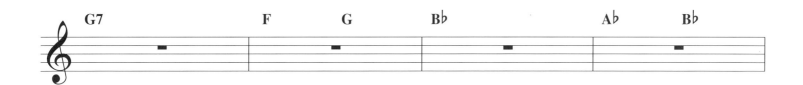

What a feel - ing. _____
(I am

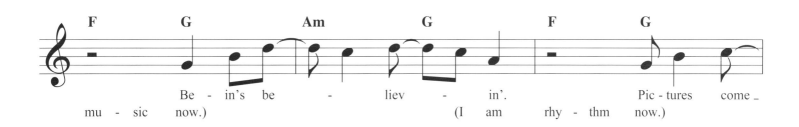

Be - in's be - liev - in'.   Pic - tures come ___
mu - sic now.)   (I am rhy - thm now.)

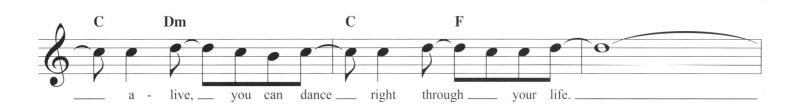

___ a - live, ___ you can dance ___ right through ___ your life. _____

Repeat and Fade

What a feel - ing. _____   What a feel -
(I can real - ly have ___ it all.)

EYE OF THE TIGER
Theme from ROCKY III

Words and Music by FRANK SULLIVAN
and JIM PETERIK

Moderately

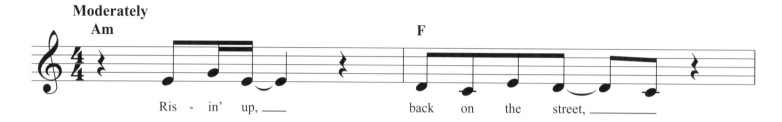

Ris - in' up, _____ back on the street, _____

did my time, _____ took my chanc - es.

Went the dis - tance; now I'm back on my feet, just a man _____

_____ and his will to sur - vive. _____

So man - y times _____ it hap - pens too fast. _____
Face to face, _____ out in the heat, _____
Ris - in' up, _____ straight to the top. _____

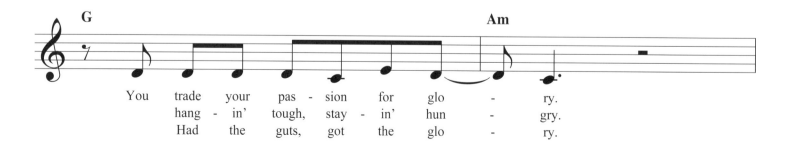

You trade your pas - sion for glo - ry.
hang - in' tough, stay - in' hun - gry.
Had the guts, got the glo - ry.

FALLING SLOWLY
from the Motion Picture ONCE

Words and Music by GLEN HANSARD
and MARKETA IRGLOVA

Slowly

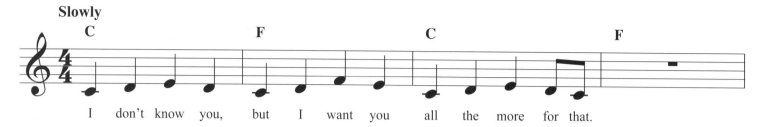

I don't know you, but I want you all the more for that.

Words fall through me and al-ways fool me, and I can't re-act.

Games that nev-er a-mount to more than they're meant will play them-selves out.

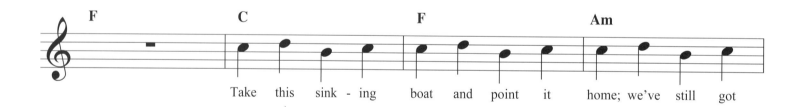

Take this sink-ing boat and point it home; we've still got

time._____ Raise your hope-ful voice; you have a choice; you make it

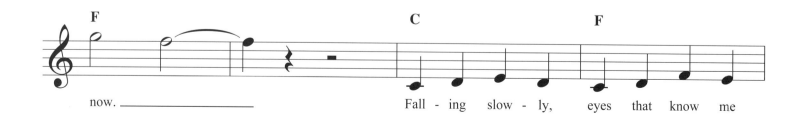

now._____ Fall-ing slow-ly, eyes that know me

and I can't go back. And moods that take me and e-rase me,

and I'm paint-ed black. Well, you have suf-fered e-nough and warred with your-

self; it's time that you won. __ Take this sink-ing

boat and point it home; we've still got time. _____ Raise your hope-ful

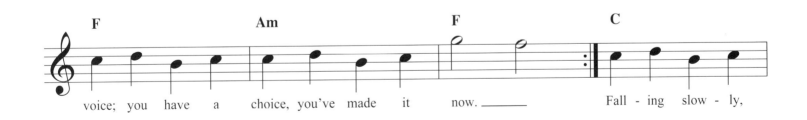

voice; you have a choice, you've made it now. _____ Fall-ing slow-ly,

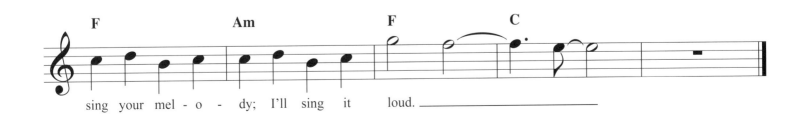

sing your mel-o-dy; I'll sing it loud. _____

FOOTLOOSE
Theme from the Paramount Motion Picture FOOTLOOSE

Words by DEAN PITCHFORD
Music by KENNY LOGGINS

Fast Rock and Roll

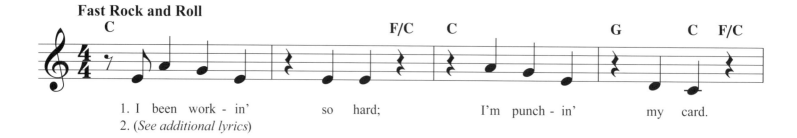

1. I been work - in' so hard; I'm punch - in' my card.
2. (*See additional lyrics*)

Eight hours, __ for what? Oh, tell me what I got.

I've got this feel - in', that time's just hold - in' me down. __

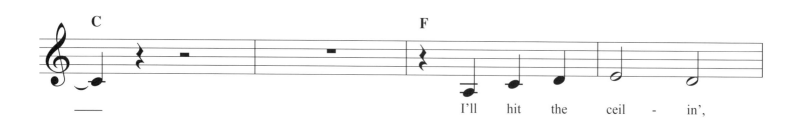

__ I'll hit the ceil - in',

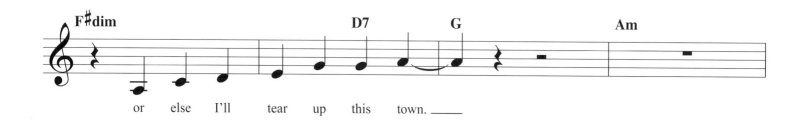

or else I'll tear up this town. __

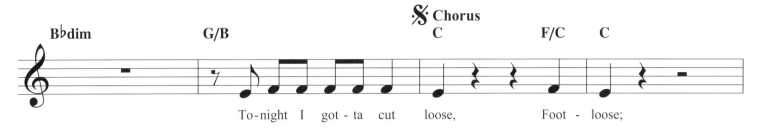

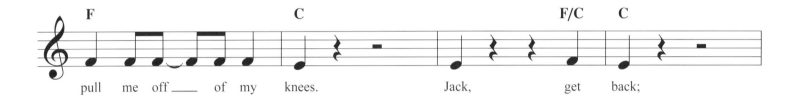

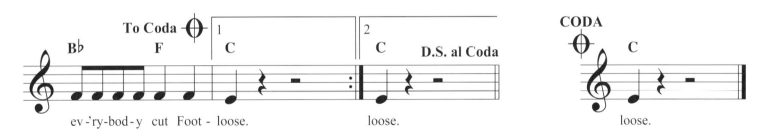

Additional Lyrics

2. You're playin' so cool
Obeying every rule
Dig way down in your heart
You're burnin', yearnin' for some…
Somebody to tell you
That life ain't a-passin' you by.
I'm tryin' to tell you
It will if you don't even try;
You can fly if you'd only cut…
Chorus

D.S. Loose, Footloose
Kick off your Sunday shoes.
Ooh-ee, Marie,
Shake it, shake it for me.
Whoa, Milo,
Come on, come on, let's go.
Lose your blues,
Everybody cut Footloose.

FORREST GUMP – MAIN TITLE
(Feather Theme)
from the Paramount Motion Picture FORREST GUMP

Music by
ALAN SILVESTRI

GHOSTBUSTERS
from the Columbia Motion Picture GHOSTBUSTERS

Words and Music by
RAY PARKER, JR.

1. If there's some-thing strange in your neigh-bor-hood,
(2.) see-ing things run-ning through your head,

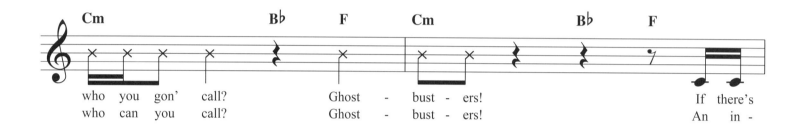

who you gon' call? Ghost - bust - ers! If there's
who can you call? Ghost - bust - ers! An in -

some-thing weird and it don't look good, who you gon' call? Ghost -
vis-i-ble man sleep-ing in your bed, who you gon' call? Ghost -

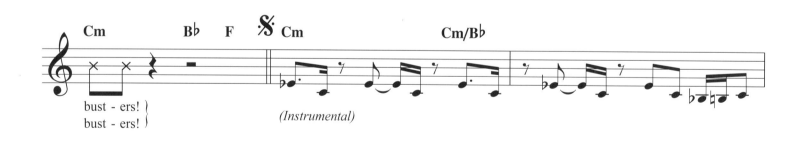

bust-ers!)
bust-ers!)
(Instrumental)

(Spoken:) I ain't 'fraid of no ghost!

I ain't 'fraid of no ghost!

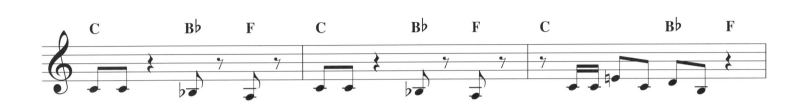

2. If you're   I ain't 'fraid of no ghost!

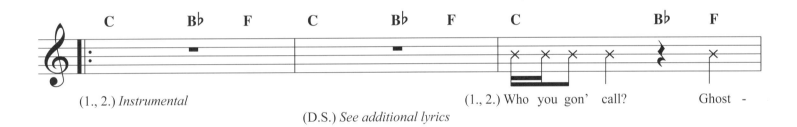

(1., 2.) Instrumental   (1., 2.) Who you gon' call?   Ghost-

(D.S.) See additional lyrics

bust - ers!   3. If you're   all a - lone,   pick   up the phone   and

4. See additional lyrics

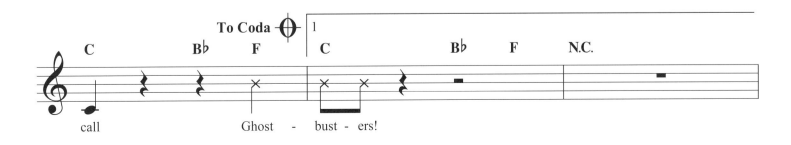

call   Ghost - bust - ers!

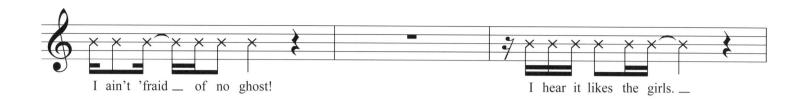

I ain't 'fraid — of no ghost!   I hear it likes the girls. —

I ain't 'fraid — of no ghost!   Yeah, yeah, yeah, yeah.

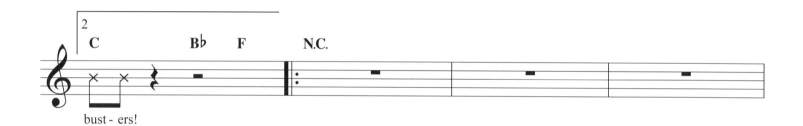

bust - ers!

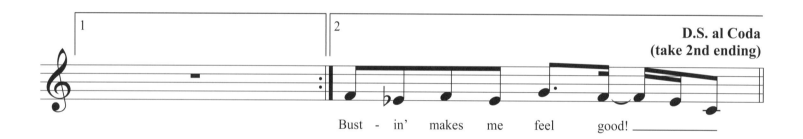

Bust - in' makes me feel good! _____

CODA

Repeat and Fade

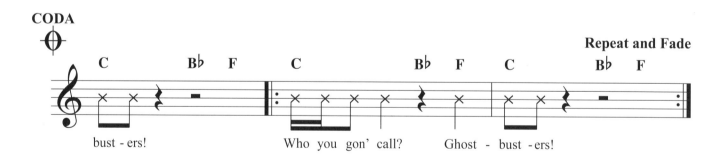

bust - ers!   Who you gon' call?   Ghost - bust -ers!

Additional Lyrics

4. Who you gon' call? *(Ghostbusters!)*
   Mm, if you have a dose of a freaky ghost, baby, you'd better call *(Ghostbusters!)*

(D.S.) Don't get caught alone, oh no. *(Ghostbusters!)*
   When it comes through your door,
   Unless you just want some more, I think you better call *(Ghostbusters!)*

GONNA FLY NOW
Theme from ROCKY

By BILL CONTI,
AYN ROBBINS and CAROL CONNORS

HALLELUJAH
featured in the DreamWorks Motion Picture SHREK

Words and Music by
LEONARD COHEN

Moderately slow, in 2

1. I've   heard   there   was   a   se - cret   chord _____   that
(2.–5.) *See additional lyrics*

Da - vid   played __   and   it   pleased   the   Lord, __   but   you   don't _____   real - ly

care   for   mu - sic, _____   do   ya? _____   It

goes   like   this: the   fourth,   the   fifth,   the   mi - nor   fall, _____   the

ma - jor   lift, _____   the   baf - fled   king __   com - pos - ing _____   Hal - le -

lu - jah. _____   Hal - le - lu - jah, _____   hal - le -

lu - jah, _____   hal - le - lu - jah, _____   hal - le -

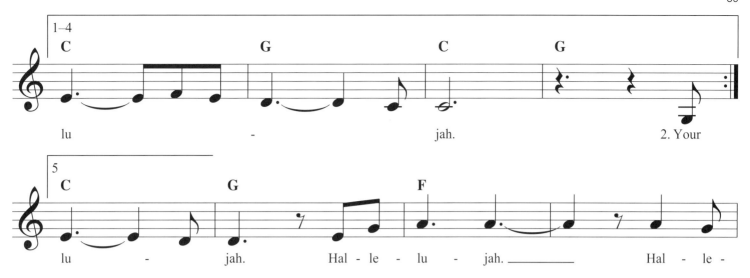

1–4

C   G   C   G

lu - jah.   2. Your

5

C   G   F

lu - jah. Hal - le - lu - jah. _____ Hal - le -

Am   F

lu - jah. _____ Hal - le - lu - jah. _____ Hal - le -

C   G   C

lu - jah. _____

Additional Lyrics

2. Your faith was strong but you needed proof.
   You saw her bathing on the roof.
   Her beauty and the moonlight overthrew ya.
   She tied you to a kitchen chair.
   She broke your throne, she cut your hair.
   And from your lips she drew the Hallelujah.

3. Maybe I have been here before.
   I know this room, I've walked this floor.
   I used to live alone before I knew ya.
   I've seen your flag on the marble arch.
   Love is not a vict'ry march.
   It's a cold and it's a broken Hallelujah.

4. There was a time you let me know
   What's real and going on below.
   But now you never show it to me, do ya?
   And remember when I moved in you.
   The holy dark was movin', too,
   And every breath we drew was Hallelujah.

5. Maybe there's a God above,
   And all I ever learned from love
   Was how to shoot at someone who outdrew ya.
   And it's not a cry you can hear at night.
   It's not somebody who's seen the light.
   It's a cold and it's a broken Hallelujah.

HAPPY
from DESPICABLE ME 2

Words and Music by
PHARRELL WILLIAMS

Moderately fast

It might seem cra - zy what I'm 'bout to say:
Here come bad news, _____ talk - in' this and that.

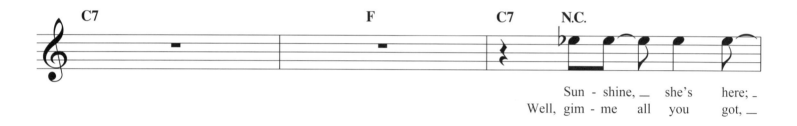

Sun - shine, _ she's here; _
Well, gim - me all you got, _

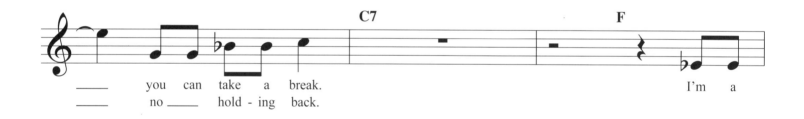

_____ you can take a break.
_____ no _____ hold - ing back.

I'm a

hot air bal - loon _____ that could go to space
Well, I should prob - 'bly warn _____ you, I'll be just _ fine.

with the air _____ like I don't care, _____ ba - by, by the way. _____
No of - fense to you, _____ don't _ waste your time. _____

92

93

I AM A MAN OF CONSTANT SORROW
featured in O BROTHER, WHERE ART THOU?

Words and Music by CARTER STANLEY
and RALPH STANLEY

Moderately fast Country

I am a man
For six long years
It's fare thee well,
You can bur - y me
May - be your friends think

of con - stant sor - row.
I've been in trou - ble,
my own true lov - er,
in some deep val - ley
I'm just a stran - ger;

I've seen trou -
no pleas - ure here
I nev - er ex - pect
for man - y years
my face you nev -

- ble all my days.
on earth I've found.
to see you a - gain,
where I may lay,
er will see no more.

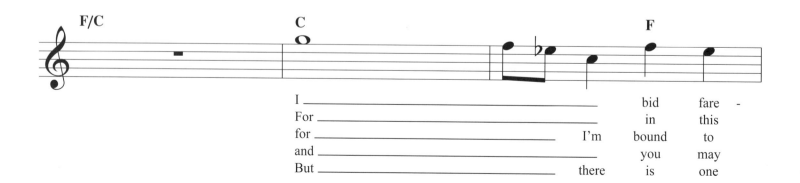

I bid fare -
For in this
for I'm bound to
and you may
But there is one

well _____ to old ___ Ken - tuck - y, _____
world _____ I'm bound _ to ram - ble; _____
ride _____ that North - ern rail - road; _____
learn _____ to love ___ an - oth - er _____
prom - ise that is giv - en: _____

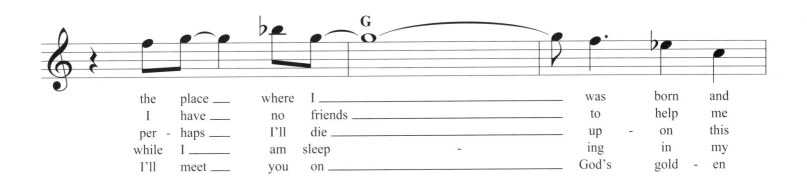

the place ___ where I _____ was born and
I have ___ no friends _____ to help me
per - haps ___ I'll die _____ up - on this
while I ___ am sleep - ing in my
I'll meet ___ you on _____ God's gold - en

raised. The place where he _____ was born and
now. He has no friends _____ to help him
train. Per - haps he'll die _____ up - on this
grave. While he is sleep - ing in his
shore. He'll meet you on _____ God's gold - en

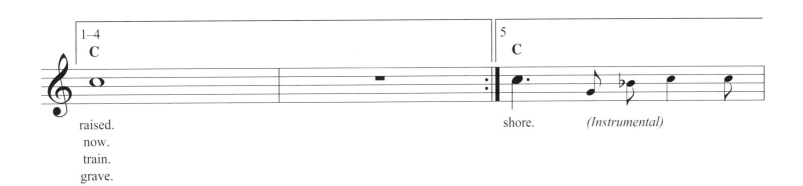

raised.
now.
train.
grave.

shore. (Instrumental)

I BELIEVE I CAN FLY
from SPACE JAM

Words and Music by
ROBERT KELLY

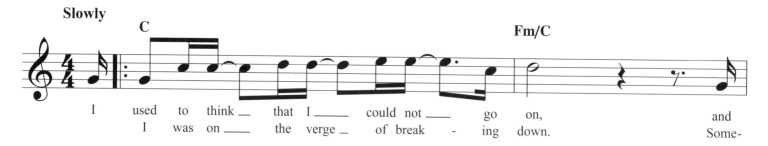

I used   to think __ that I ____ could not ____   go   on,   and
I was   on ___   the verge __ of break - ing   down.   Some-

life   was noth -   ing but __   an aw - ful   song. _____   But
times si -   lence __ can seem __ so   loud. _____   There are

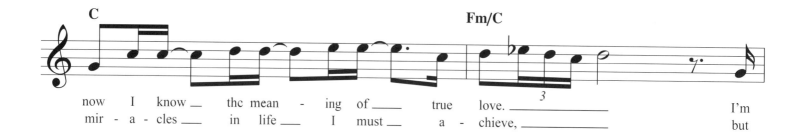

now I know __ the mean - ing of ____ true   love. _____   I'm
mir - a - cles __   in life ___ I must __ a - chieve, _____   but

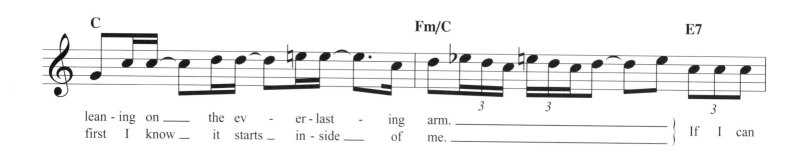

lean - ing on ____ the ev - er - last - ing   arm. _____   If   I can
first I know __ it starts __ in - side ___ of   me. _____   If   I can

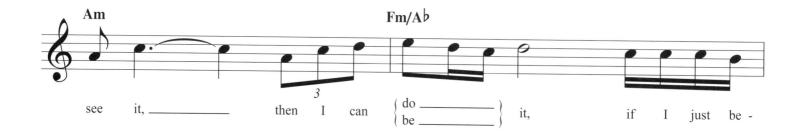

see   it, _____   then I can { do _____ } it,   if   I just be-
                                              { be _____ }

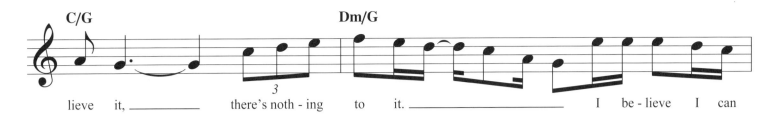

lieve it, _____ there's noth - ing to it. _____ I be - lieve I can

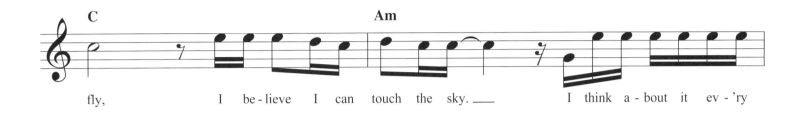

fly, I be - lieve I can touch the sky. ___ I think a - bout it ev - 'ry

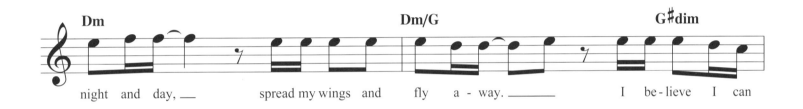

night and day, ___ spread my wings and fly a - way. _____ I be - lieve I can

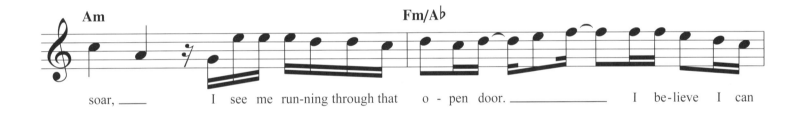

soar, ___ I see me run-ning through that o - pen door. _____ I be-lieve I can

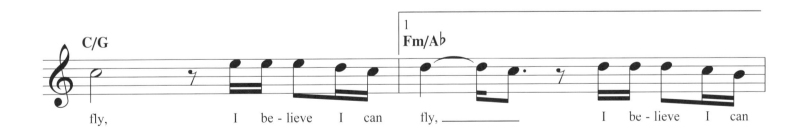

fly, I be - lieve I can fly, _____ I be - lieve I can

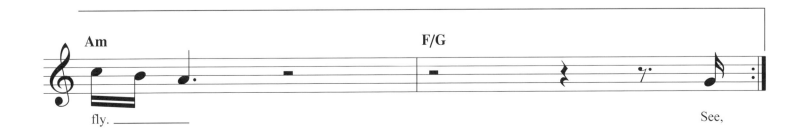

fly. _____ See,

fly, _____ oh, I be - lieve I can fly. _____

Hey, _____ 'cause I be - lieve ___ in me, _____ oh. _____

_____ If I can see it, then I can

do _____ it, if I just be - lieve it, _____ there's noth - ing

to it. _____ I be - lieve I can fly, I be - lieve I can

touch the sky. ___ I think a - bout it ev - ery night and day, ___ spread my wings and

99

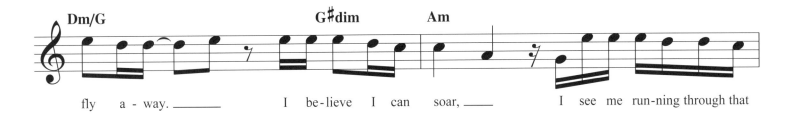

fly a - way. _____ I be-lieve I can soar, _____ I see me run-ning through that

o - pen door. _____ I be-lieve I can fly, I be-lieve I can

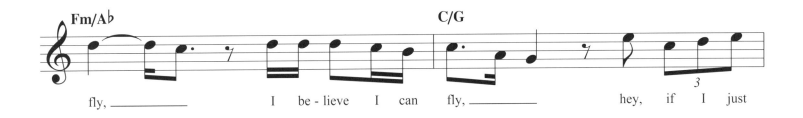

fly, _____ I be-lieve I can fly, _____ hey, if I just

spread my wings. _____ I can fly, I can fly, _____ I can

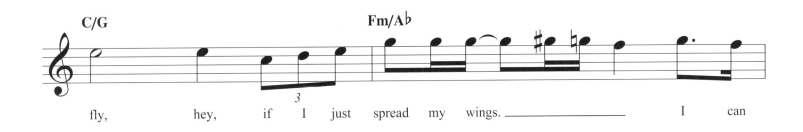

fly, hey, if I just spread my wings. _____ I can

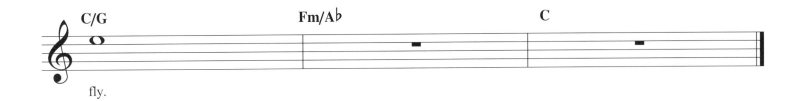

fly.

I WALK THE LINE
featured in WALK THE LINE

Words and Music by
JOHN R. CASH

Moderately bright

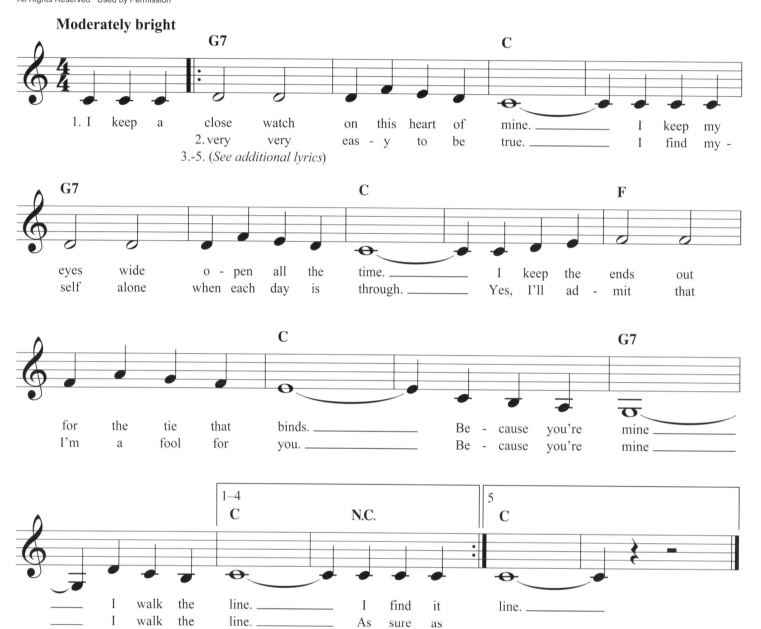

Additional Lyrics

3. As sure as night is dark and day is light,
   I keep you on my mind both day and night.
   And happiness I've known proves that it's right.
   Because you're mine I walk the line.

4. You've got a way to keep me on your side.
   You give me cause for love that I can't hide.
   For you I know I'd even try to turn the tide.
   Because you're mine I walk the line.

5. I keep a close watch on this heart of mine.
   I keep my eyes wide open all the time.
   I keep the ends out for the tie that binds.
   Because you're mine I walk the line.

I WILL ALWAYS LOVE YOU
featured in THE BODYGUARD

Words and Music by
DOLLY PARTON

And I _____ will _____ al - ways

love you. _____ I will _____ al - ways

love you. _____ You, _____ my

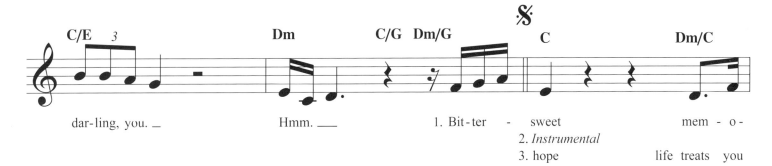

dar - ling, you. _   Hmm. ___   1. Bit - ter - sweet   mem - o -
2. *Instrumental*
3. hope   life treats you

ries   that is ____ all _____ I'm tak - ing ____ with
kind,   and I ____ hope ____ you have _ all ___ you've

me. _____ So, good - bye. _____ Please,
dreamed _____ of. _____ And I wish _ to you   joy

102

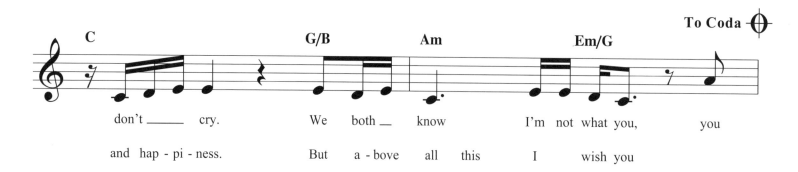

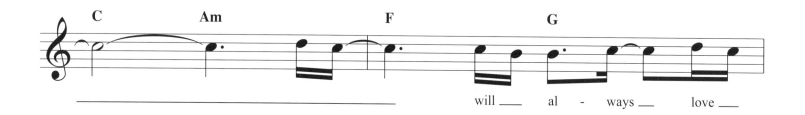

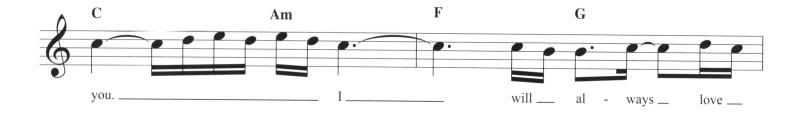

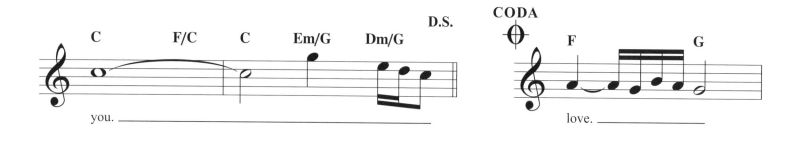

you. _____ I will al - ways _____ love ___

you. I _____ will al - ways _____ love _ you. _____ I will al -

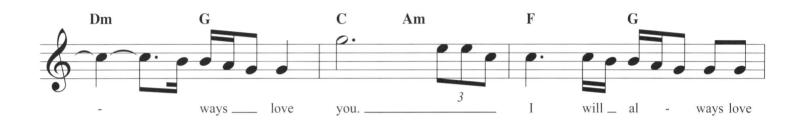

- ways ____ love you. _____ I will _ al - ways love

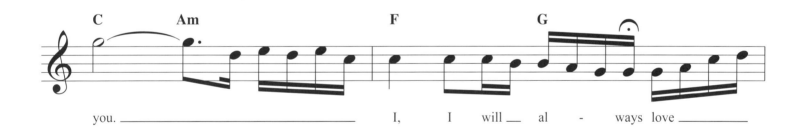

you. _____ I, I will _ al - ways love _____

you. _____ You, _____ dar - ling, I love _ you. Ooh, _____ I'll __

al - ways, I'll _ al - ways ____ love _____ you. _____

I WILL WAIT FOR YOU
from THE UMBRELLAS OF CHERBOURG

Music by MICHEL LEGRAND
Original French Text by JACQUES DEMY
English Words by NORMAN GIMBEL

Moderately

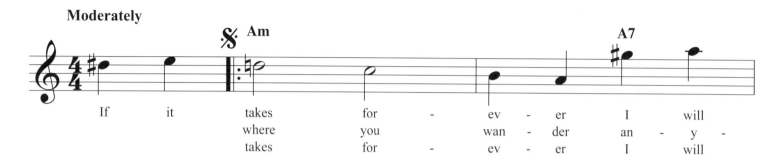

If it takes for - ev - er I will
where you wan - der an - y -
takes for - ev - er I will

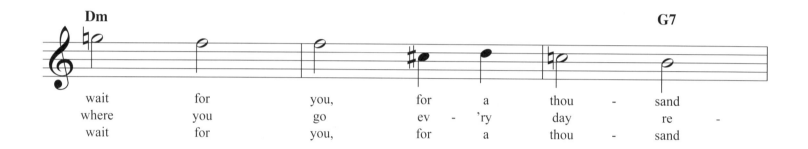

wait for you, for a thou - sand
where you go ev - 'ry day re -
wait for you, for a thou - sand

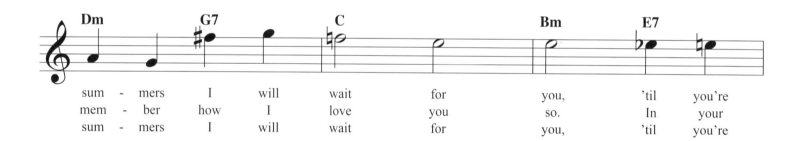

sum - mers I will wait for you, 'til you're
mem - ber how I love you so. In your
sum - mers I will wait for you, 'til you're

back be - side me 'til I'm hold - ing
heart be - lieve what in my heart I
here be - side me 'til I'm touch - ing

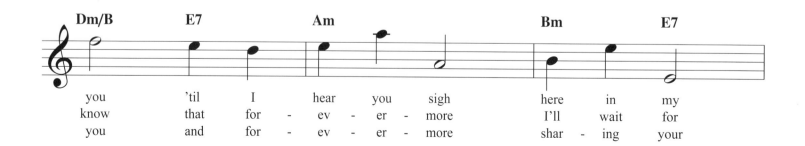

you 'til I hear you sigh here in my
know that for - ev - er - more I'll wait for
you and for - ev - er - more shar - ing your

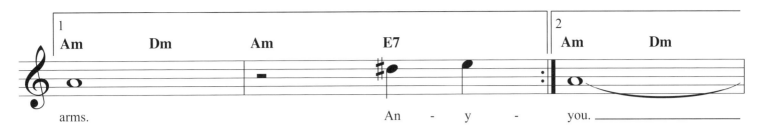

arms.   An - y -   you.

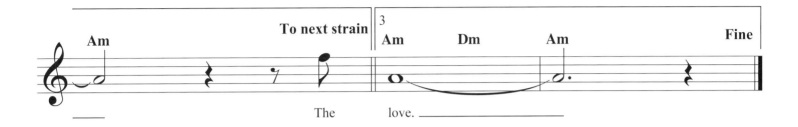

To next strain   Fine

The   love.

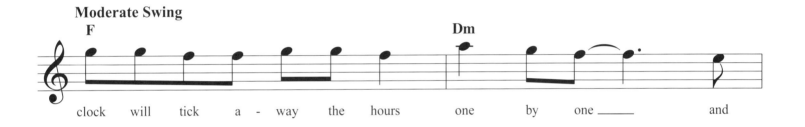

clock will tick a - way the hours one by one ____ and

then the time will come when all the wait - ing's done. ____ The

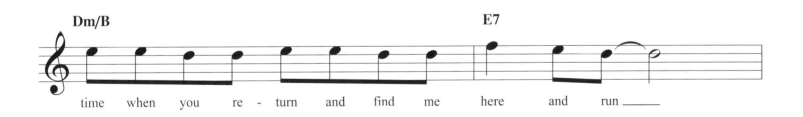

time when you re - turn and find me here and run ____

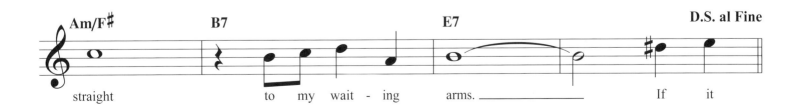

straight   to my wait - ing arms. ____ If it

IF I WERE A RICH MAN
from the Musical FIDDLER ON THE ROOF

Words by SHELDON HARNICK
Music by JERRY BOCK

(Instrumental)

IT MUST HAVE BEEN LOVE

featured in the Motion Picture PRETTY WOMAN

Words and Music by
PER GESSLE

108

IL POSTINO
(The Postman)
from IL POSTINO

Music by LUIS BACALOV

Slowly

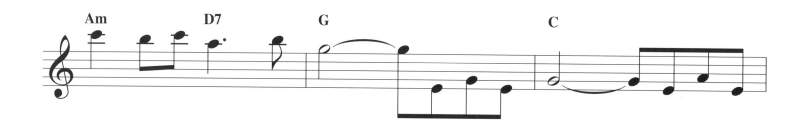

THEME FROM "JAWS"
from the Universal Picture JAWS

By JOHN WILLIAMS

KOKOMO
from the Motion Picture COCKTAIL

Words and Music by JOHN PHILLIPS,
TERRY MELCHER, MIKE LOVE
and SCOTT McKENZIE

Moderately bright

A - ru - ba, Ja - mai - ca, oo ____ I wan-na take ya. Ber - mu - da, Ba - ha - ma, come ___

____ on, pret - ty ma - ma. Key Lar - go, Mon - te - go, ba - by, why don't we go, Ja -

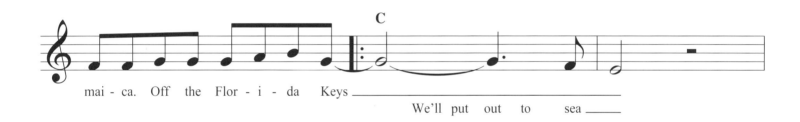

mai - ca. Off the Flor - i - da Keys ____ We'll put out to sea ____

there's a place called Ko - ko - mo. ____ That's where we
and we'll per - fect our chem - is - try. ____ By and by we'll de - fy ___

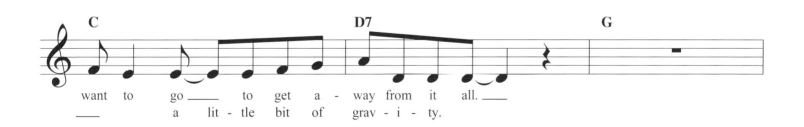

want to go ____ to get a - way from it all. ____
____ a lit - tle bit of grav - i - ty.

Bod - ies in the sand, ____ trop - i - cal drink melt - ing
Af - ter - noon de - light, ____ cock - tails and

in your hand. __ We'll be fall-ing in love ____ to the rhy-thm of a
moon-lit nights. __ The dream-y look in your eye, ____ give me a trop-i-cal

steel drum band ____ down in Ko-ko-mo. } A - ru - ba, Ja - mai - ca, oo __
con-tact high ____ way down in Ko-ko-mo. }

__ I wan-na take you to Ber - mu-da, Ba-ha-ma. Come __ on, pret-ty ma-ma. Key

Lar - go, Mon-te-go, ba - by, why don't we go down to Ko-ko - mo. __ We'll

get there fast ____ and then we'll take it slow. __ That's where __ we __

wan-na go, ____ way down in Ko-ko - mo. { Mar - tin - ique, that
{ Port Au Prince, I

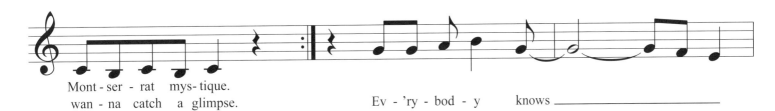

THE JOHN DUNBAR THEME
from DANCES WITH WOLVES

By JOHN BARRY

118

LET IT GO
from FROZEN

Music and Lyrics by KRISTEN ANDERSON-LOPEZ
and ROBERT LOPEZ

al - ways have __ to be.   Con - ceal, __ don't feel,   don't let __ them know... __

_____ Well, now ___ they know. _____ Let it go, __

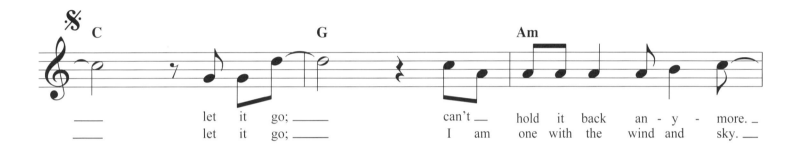

___ let it go; ___   can't ___ hold it back   an - y - more. __
___ let it go; ___   I am one with the wind and sky. __

___ Let it go, ___   let it go; ___   turn a - way __
___ Let it go, ___   let it go; ___   you'll __ nev -

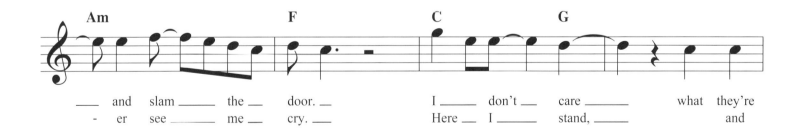

___ and slam ___ the __ door. ___   I ___ don't __ care _____   what they're
- er see ___ me __ cry. __   Here __ I _____ stand, _____   and

going   to ___ say; _____   let the storm rage ___ on. _____   The
here   I'll ___ stay; _____   let the storm rage ___ on. __

Gaining confidence

cold nev - er both-ered me an - y - way. *(Instrumental)*

It's fun - ny how some dis - tance makes

ev - 'ry-thing __ seem small; __ and the fears that once __ con - trolled __ me can't

get to me __ at all. __ It's time __ to see __ what I __ can do,

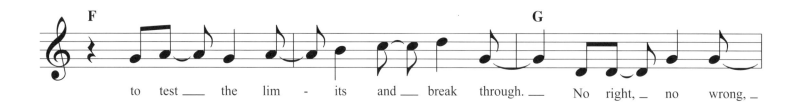

to test __ the lim - its and __ break through. __ No right, __ no wrong, __

D.S. al Coda

__ no rules __ for me, __ I'm free! _____ Let it go, __

CODA

My pow - er flur - ries through _ the air _

_ in - to _ the ground. _ My soul _ is spi -

- ral - ing _ in fro - zen frac - tals all _ a - round. _

And one _ thought crys - tal - liz - es like _ an i - cy blast: _

_ I'm nev - er go - ing back; _ the

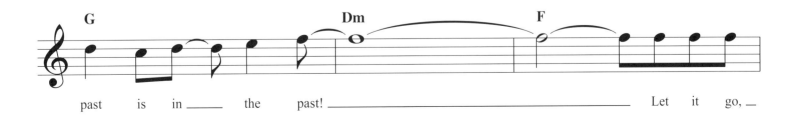

past is in _ the past! _____ Let it go, _

let it go, _____ and I'll rise ____ like the break _ of dawn. _

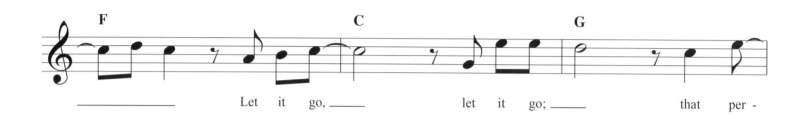

_____ Let it go, ____ let it go; ____ that per -

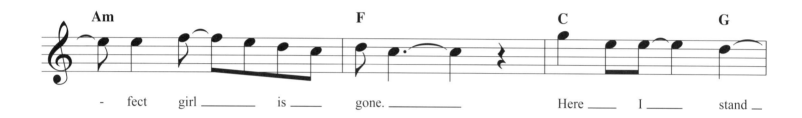

- fect girl _____ is ____ gone. _____ Here ____ I ____ stand _

____ in the light ____ of ____ day; _____

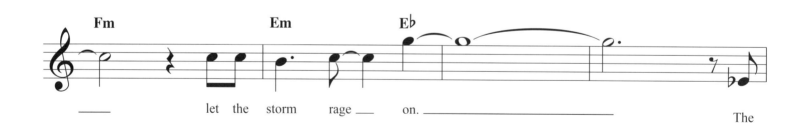

____ let the storm rage ___ on. _____ The

cold nev - er both - ered me an - y - way.

LET THE RIVER RUN
Theme from the Motion Picture WORKING GIRL

Words and Music by
CARLY SIMON

Let the riv-er run, let all the dream-ers wake the

na - tion. Come, ___ the new Je-ru-sa-

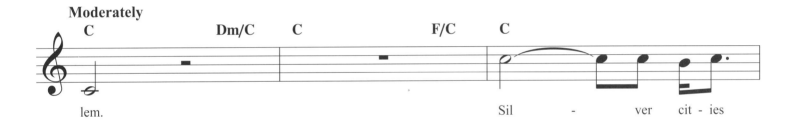

lem. Sil - ver cit-ies

rise; the morn-ing lights the streets that lead them. And

si - rens call them on with a song.

It's ask - ing for the tak - ing,

124

trem - bling, sha - ak - ing. ___ Oh, ___ my heart is

ach - ing. We're com - ing to the edge, run - ning on the wa - ter,

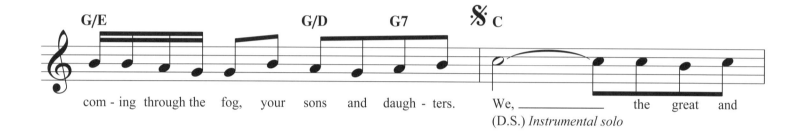

com - ing through the fog, your sons and daugh - ters. We, ___ the great and
(D.S.) *Instrumental solo*

small, ___ stand on the star and blaze a trail ___ of de -

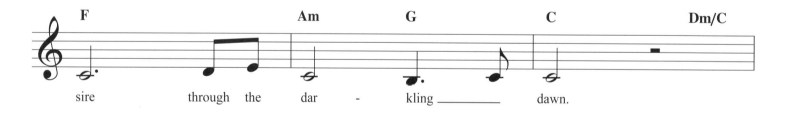

sire through the dar - kling ___ dawn.

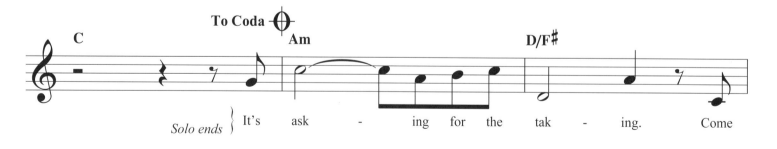

Solo ends It's ask - ing for the tak - ing. Come

run with me now; the sky is the col - or of blue you've nev - er e - ven seen in the eyes of your

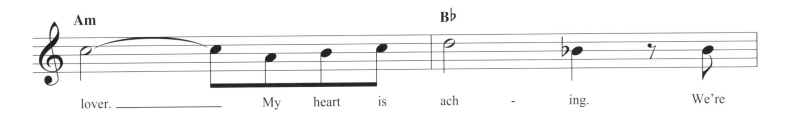

lover. _____ My heart is ach - ing. We're

D.S. al Coda

com-ing to the edge, run - ning on the wa - ter, com-ing through the fog, your sons and daugh - ters.

CODA

ask - ing for the tak - ing, trem - bling,

sha - ak - ing. __ Oh, _____ my heart is ach - ing. We're

com-ing to the edge, run - ning on the wa - ter, com-ing through the fog, your sons and daugh -ters.

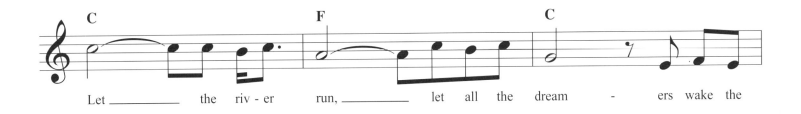

Let _____ the riv - er run, _____ let all the dream - ers wake the

na - tion. Come, ____ the new Je - ru - sa - lem.

LIVE AND LET DIE
from LIVE AND LET DIE

Words and Music by PAUL McCARTNEY
and LINDA McCARTNEY

Slowly

When you were young   and your   heart   was an o - pen book, —
Instrumental   *Instrumental ends*

you used to say   live and let   live.
You used to say   live and let   live.
(You know you did, you know you did, you know you

did.) —   But if this ev - er - chang - ing   world   in   which we   live in   makes you

give   in and cry, —   say live and let   die! —   Live and let

die, —   live and let   die, —   live and let   die. —

(Instrumental)

To Coda

What does it mat - ter to ya? When you got a job to do, you got - ta

do it well. You got - ta give the oth - er fel - low hell! _____

_____ *(Instrumental)*

D.C. al Coda

CODA

THE LOOK OF LOVE
from CASINO ROYALE

Words and Music by HAL DAVID
and BURT BACHARACH

Moderately

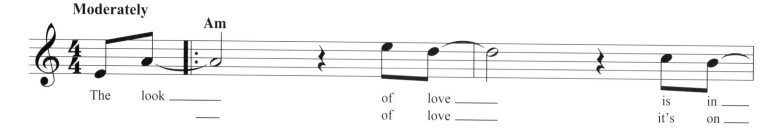

The look _____ of love _____ is in _____
of love _____ it's on _____

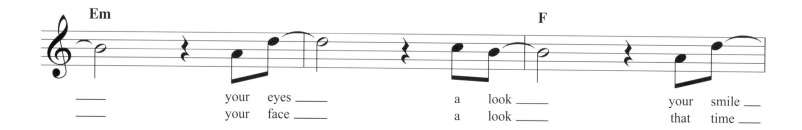

_____ your eyes _____ a look _____ your smile ___
_____ your face _____ a look _____ that time ___

_____ can't dis - guise. _____ The look ___
_____ can't e - rase. _____ Be mine _

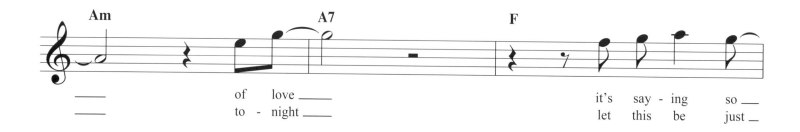

_____ of love _____ it's say - ing so ___
_____ to - night _____ let this be just _

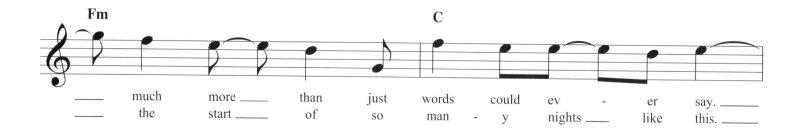

_____ much more _____ than just words could ev - er say. _____
_____ the start _____ of so man - y nights _____ like this. _____

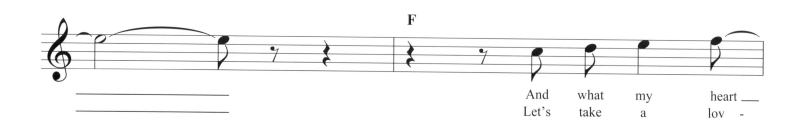

_____ And what my heart ___
_____ Let's take a lov -

has heard, ___ well, it takes my breath ___ a - way. ___
- er's vow ___ and then seal it with ___ a kiss. ___

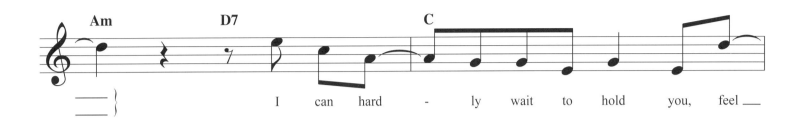

___ I can hard - ly wait to hold you, feel ___

___ my arms a - round you, how long ___ I have wait - ed,

wait - ed just to love you, now ___ that I have found you, ___

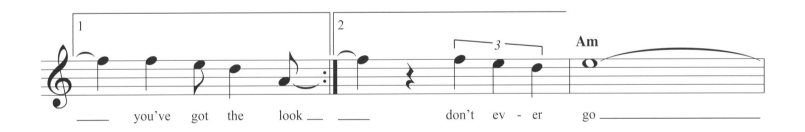

___ you've got the look ___ don't ev - er go ___

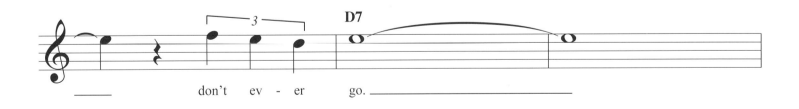

___ don't ev - er go. ___

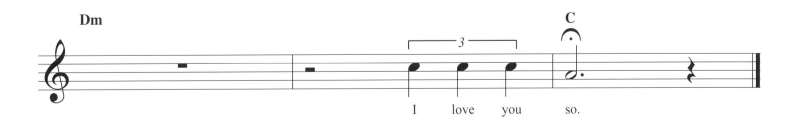

I love you so.

A MAN AND A WOMAN
(Un Homme Et Une Femme)
from A MAN AND A WOMAN

Original Words by PIERRE BAROUH
English Words by JERRY KELLER
Music by FRANCIS LAI

Moderately

When hearts are pass-ing in the night, in the lone-ly night ___
si-lence of the mist, of the morn-ing mist, ___

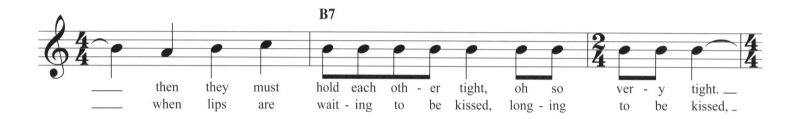

___ then they must hold each oth-er tight, oh so ver-y tight. ___
___ when lips are wait-ing to be kissed, long-ing to be kissed, _

___ And take a chance that in the light in to-mor-row's light _____ they'll stay to-
___ where is the rea-son to re-sist and de-ny a kiss _____ that holds a

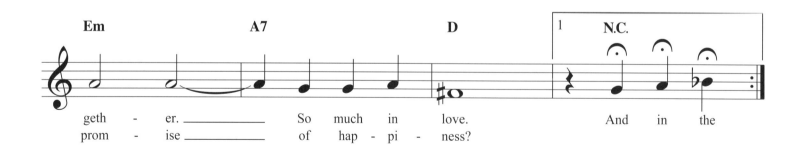

geth - er. _____ So much in love. And in the
prom - ise _____ of hap-pi-ness?

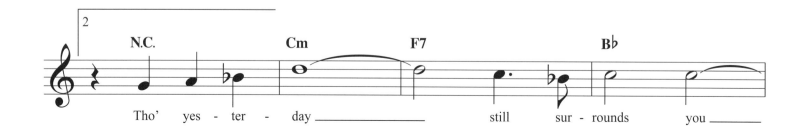

Tho' yes-ter-day _____ still sur-rounds you _____

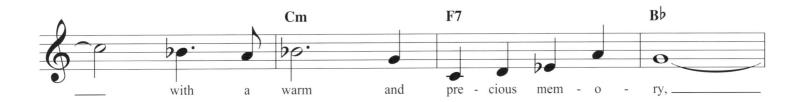

with a warm and pre-cious mem-o-ry, _____

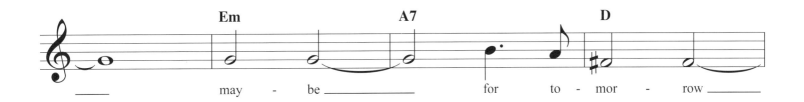

_____ may-be _____ for to-mor-row _____

_____ we can build a new dream _____ for you and me.

This glow we / feel is some-thing rare, some-thing real-ly rare. ___
pass-ing in the night, in the rush-ing night. ___

_____ So, come and / say you want to share, want to real-ly share ___
_____ A man, a wom-an in the night, in the lone-ly night ___

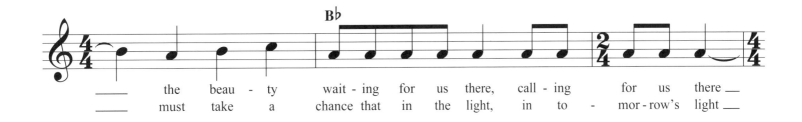

_____ the beau-ty / wait-ing for us there, call-ing for us there ___
_____ must take a / chance that in the light, in-to-mor-row's light ___

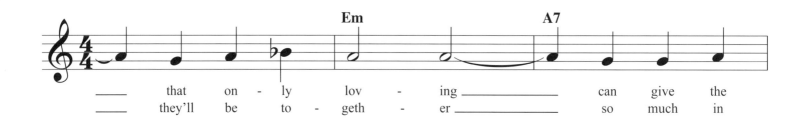

that on - ly lov - ing _____ can give the
they'll be to - geth - er _____ so much in

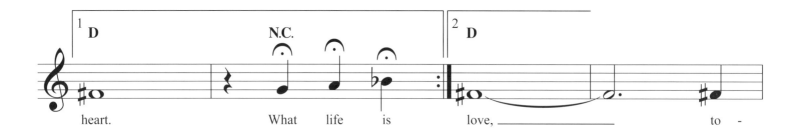

heart. What life is love, _____ to -

geth - er _____ so much in love. _____ So,

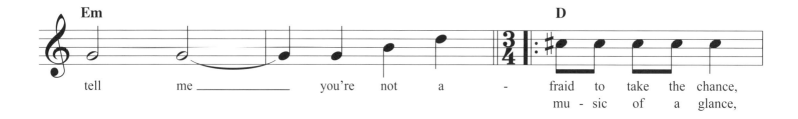

tell me _____ you're not a - fraid to take the chance,
mu - sic of a glance,

real - ly take a chance. Let your heart be - gin to dance,
of a fleet - ing glance, to the mu - sic of ro - mance,

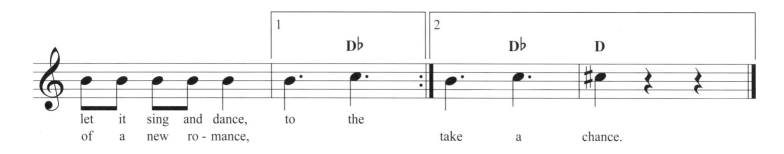

let it sing and dance, to the
of a new ro - mance, take a chance.

THEME FROM "NEW YORK, NEW YORK"
from NEW YORK, NEW YORK

Words by FRED EBB
Music by JOHN KANDER

(Instrumental)

Start spread-in' the news,   I'm leav-ing to-

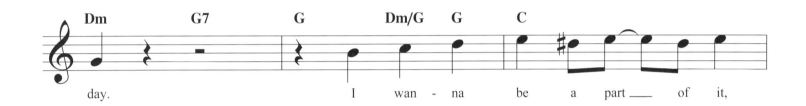

day.   I wan-na be a part __ of it,

New York, New York.   These vag-a-bond

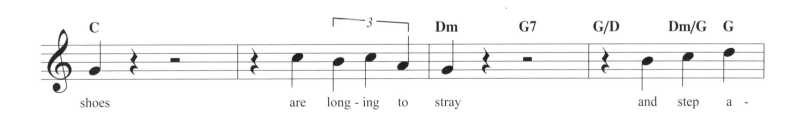

shoes   are long-ing to stray   and step a-

round the heart __ of it,   New York, New York. _____ I wan-na
(D.S.) (Instrumental)

To Coda

A MILLION DREAMS
from THE GREATEST SHOWMAN

Words and Music by BENJ PASEK
and JUSTIN PAUL

Moderately, with intensity

I close my eyes ____ and I can see ____ a world that's wait -
There's a house ____ we can build ____ Ev - 'ry room ____

- ing up for me ____ that I call my own
____ in - side is filled ____ with things from far a - way

Through the dark, ____ through the door, ____ through where no ____
Spe - cial things ____ I com - pile, ____ each one there ____

____ one's been be - fore, ____ but it feels like home
____ to make you smile ____ on a rain - y day

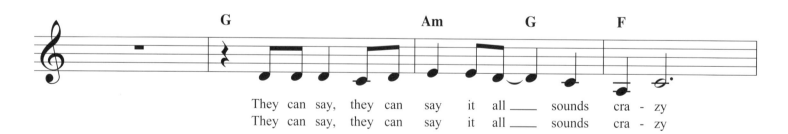

They can say, they can say it all ____ sounds cra - zy
They can say, they can say it all ____ sounds cra - zy

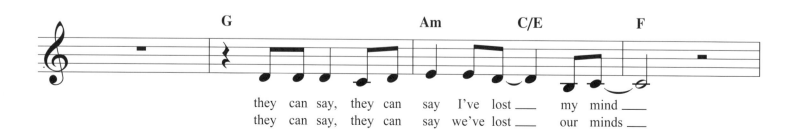

they can say, they can say I've lost ____ my mind ____
they can say, they can say we've lost ____ our minds ____

I don't care, I don't care, so call me cra - zy
I don't care, I don't care if they call us cra - zy

We can live in a world that we __ de - sign __
Run a - way to a world that we __ de - sign __

'Cause ev - 'ry night __ I lie __ in bed __ the bright - est col - ors fill __

__ my head A mil - lion dreams __ are keep - in' me __ a - wake __

I think of what __ the world __ could be, __ a

vi - sion of __ the one __ I see A mil - lion dreams __ is all __

__ it's gon - na take __ Oh, a mil - lion dreams __ for the

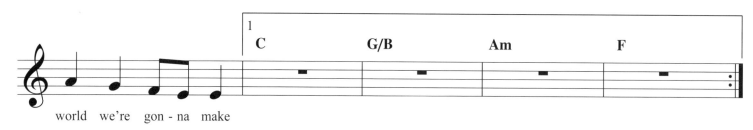

world we're gon - na make

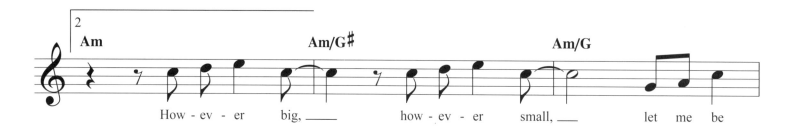

How - ev - er big, ___ how - ev - er small, ___ let me be

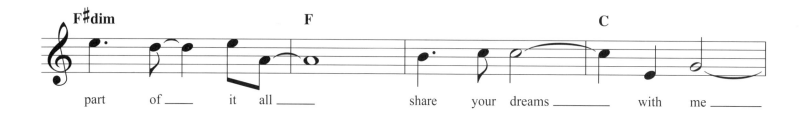

part of ___ it all ___ share your dreams ___ with me ___

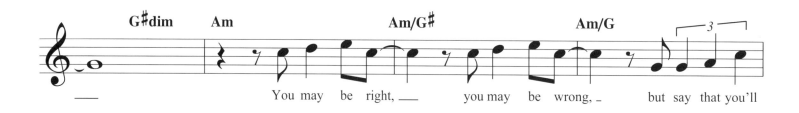

___ You may be right, ___ you may be wrong, _ but say that you'll

bring me ___ a - long ___ to the world you ___ see, ___ to the

world I close my eyes to see, ___ I close my eyes to see ___

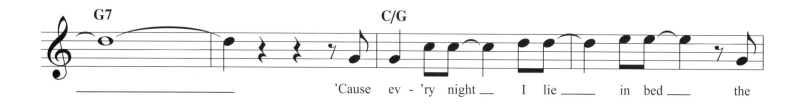

_____ 'Cause ev - 'ry night _ I lie ___ in bed ___ the

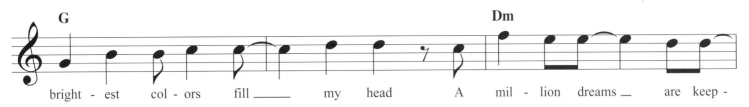

bright - est col - ors fill _____ my head A mil - lion dreams _ are keep -

- in' me ___ a - wake ___ I think of what _ the world _

___ could be, ___ a vi - sion of ___ the one ___ I see A

mil - lion dreams _ is all ___ it's gon - na take ___

A mil - lion dreams _ for the world we're gon - na make _____

_____ For the world we're gon - na make

(Instrumental)

MRS. ROBINSON
from THE GRADUATE

Words and Music by
PAUL SIMON

141

you for ___ our files. ___ We'd like to help ___ you

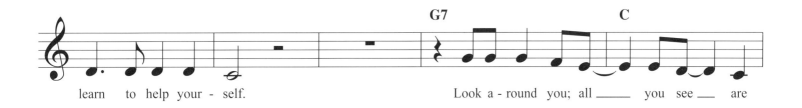

learn to help your-self. Look a-round you; all ___ you see ___ are

sym - pa-thet - ic eyes. ___ Stroll a-round ___

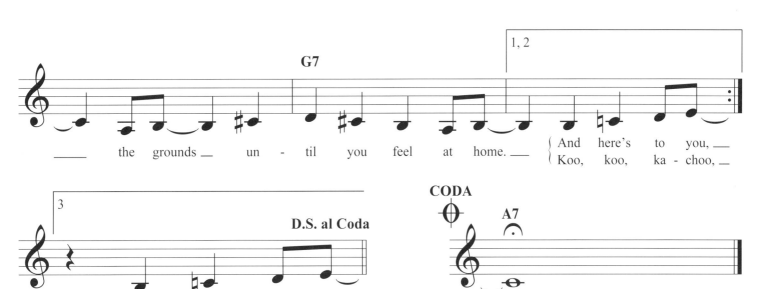

___ the grounds ___ un - til you feel at home. ___ { And here's to you, ___ / Koo, koo, ka - choo, ___

Where have you gone, _

___

Additional Lyrics

2. Hide it in a hiding place where no one ever goes.
   Put it in your pantry with your cupcakes.
   It's a little secret, just the Robinsons' affair.
   Most of all, you've got to hide it from the kids.

3. Sitting on a sofa on a Sunday afternoon,
   Going to the candidates' debate.
   Laugh about it, shout about it when you've got to choose.
   Ev'ry way you look at this, you lose.

Last Chorus: Where have you gone, Joe DiMaggio?
   A nation turns its lonely eyes to you, woo, woo, woo.
   What's that you say, Mrs. Robinson?
   Joltin' Joe has left and gone away,
   Hey, hey, hey, hey, hey, hey.

MOON RIVER

from the Paramount Picture BREAKFAST AT TIFFANY'S

Words by JOHNNY MERCER
Music by HENRY MANCINI

Slow Waltz

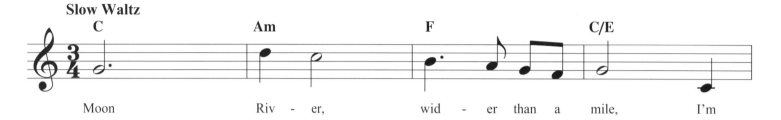

Moon Riv - er, wid - er than a mile, I'm

cross - in' you in style some day._____ Old

dream - mak - er, you heart - break - er, wher -

ev - er you're go - in',___ I'm go - in' ___ your way.

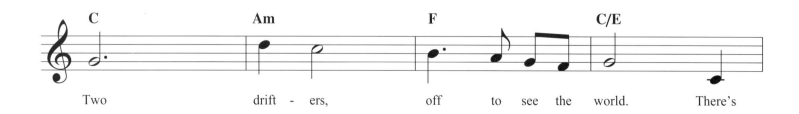

Two drift - ers, off to see the world. There's

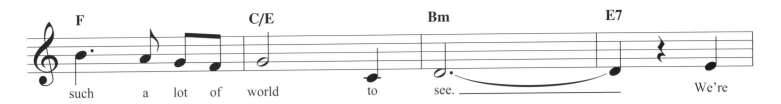

such a lot of world to see. _____ We're

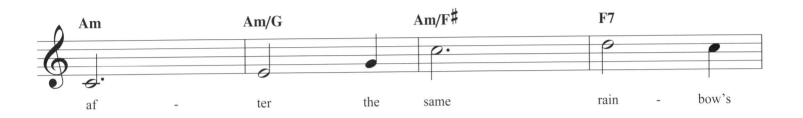

af - ter the same rain - bow's

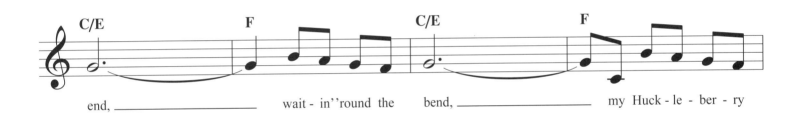

end, _____ wait - in' 'round the bend, _____ my Huck - le - ber - ry

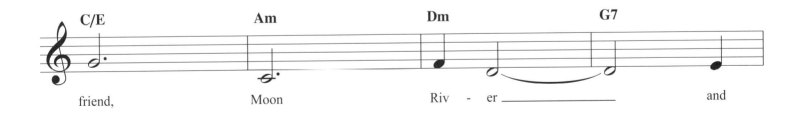

friend, Moon Riv - er _____ and

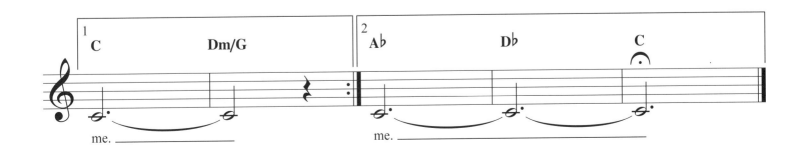

me. _____ me.

MORE
(Ti Guarderò Nel Cuore)
from the film MONDO CANE

Music by NINO OLIVIERO and RIZ ORTOLANI
Italian Lyrics by MARCELLO CIORCIOLINI
English Lyrics by NORMAN NEWELL

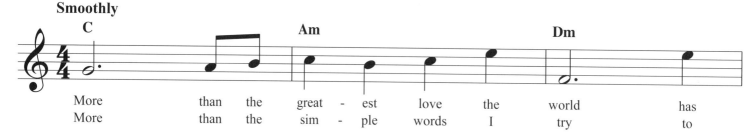

More than the great-est love the world has
More than the sim-ple love words I try to

known; this is the love I'll give to
say; I on-ly live to give love to you

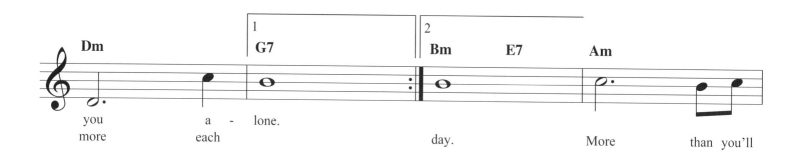

you a-lone. day. More than you'll
more each

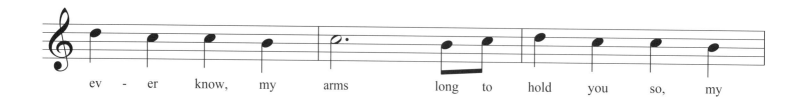

ev-er know, my arms long to hold you so, my

life will be in your keep-ing wak-ing, sleep-ing,

laugh - ing, weep - ing. Long - er than al - ways is a

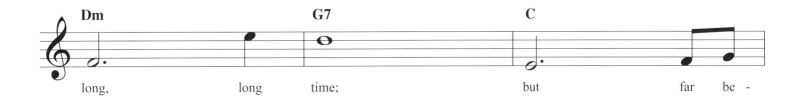

long, long time; but far be -

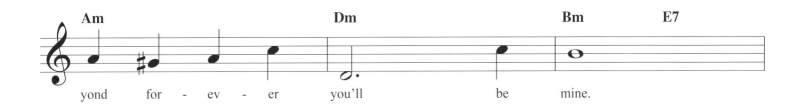

yond for - ev - er you'll be mine.

I know I nev - er lived be - fore and my

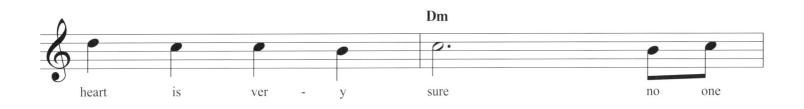

heart is ver - y sure no one

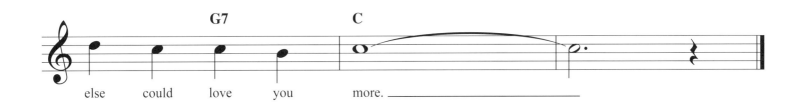

else could love you more.

THE MUSIC OF GOODBYE

from OUT OF AFRICA

Words and Music by JOHN BARRY,
ALAN BERGMAN and MARILYN BERGMAN

Medium slow Ballad

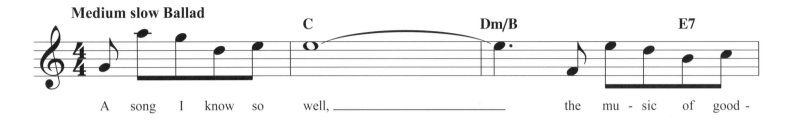

A song I know so well, _____ the mu-sic of good-

bye a - gain. _____ It's there each time we say "hel - lo." _____

_____ As al - ways there's no rea - son why a - gain. _____

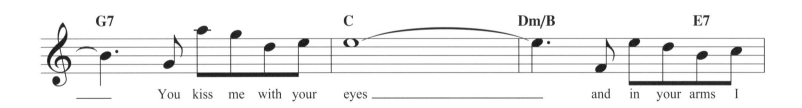

_____ You kiss me with your eyes _____ and in your arms I

fly a - gain. _____ But e - ven as we touch the clouds, _____

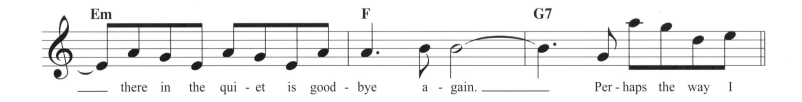

_____ there in the qui - et is good - bye a - gain. _____ Per - haps the way I

147

hold you _____ makes you a-fraid I'll hold you; _____ makes you a-fraid to

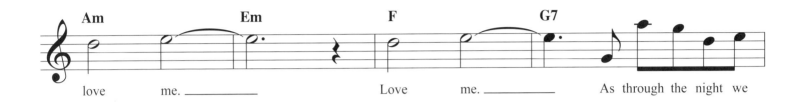

love me. _____ Love me. _____ As through the night we

dance, _____ the ten - der dance of try a - gain, _____

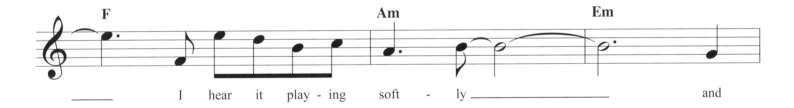

_____ I hear it play - ing soft - ly _____ and

sad - ly: _____ The mu - sic of good - bye. _____

Per-haps the way I bye. _____ Good-

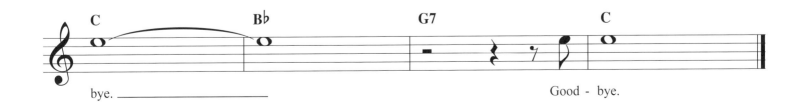

bye. _____ Good - bye.

MY HEART WILL GO ON
(Love Theme from 'Titanic')
from the Paramount and Twentieth Century Fox Motion Picture TITANIC

Music by JAMES HORNER
Lyric by WILL JENNINGS

Moderately

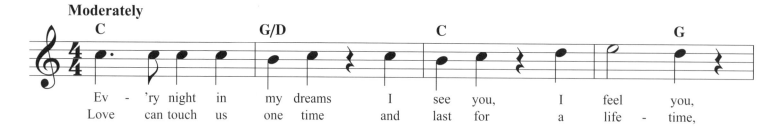

Ev - 'ry night in my dreams I see you, I feel you,
Love can touch us one time and last for a life - time,

that is how I know you go on.
and nev - er let go till we're gone.

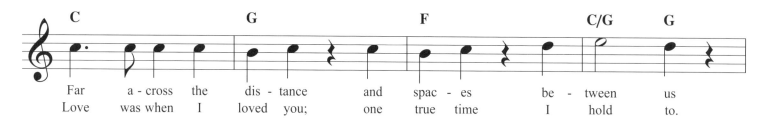

Far a - cross the dis - tance and spac - es be - tween us
Love was when I loved you; one true time I hold to.

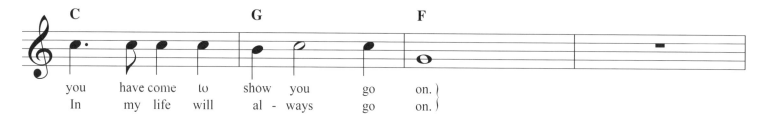

you have come to show you go on.)
In my life will al - ways go on.)

Near, far, wher - ev - er you are, ____ I be-

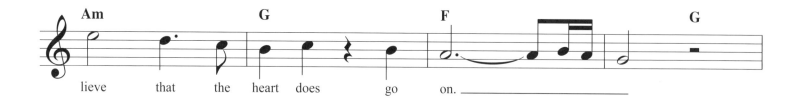

lieve that the heart does go on. ____

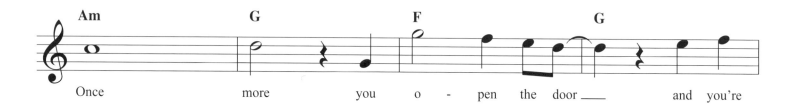

Once more you o - pen the door ____ and you're

149

NINE TO FIVE
from NINE TO FIVE

Words and Music by
DOLLY PARTON

Lively

Tum - ble out of bed and stum - ble to the kitch - en; pour my - self a cup __
let __ you __ dream just to watch __ them __ shat - ter; you're just a step on the

__ of am - bi - tion, and yawn, and stretch, and try to come __ to life. ____
boss __ man's lad - der, but you've got dreams he'll nev - er take __ a - way. ____

Jump in the show - er, and the blood starts pump - ing; out on the street, the traf -
In the same boat __ with a lot of your friends; __ wait - in' for the day your ship -

- fic starts jump-ing, with folks __ like me on the job from nine to five.
- 'll come in, __ and the tide's gon-na turn and it's all gon-na roll your way.

To Coda

Work - ing nine to ____ five, _____ what a
Work - ing Nine to ____ five, _____ for

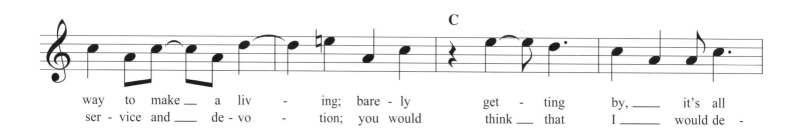

way to make __ a liv - ing; bare - ly get - ting by, __ it's all
ser - vice and __ de - vo - tion; you would think __ that I __ would de -

OH, PRETTY WOMAN

featured in the Motion Picture PRETTY WOMAN

Words and Music by ROY ORBISON
and BILL DEES

Moderate Rock

Pret - ty wom - an yeah, yeah, yeah. _____

Pret - ty wom - an look my way, _____ pret - ty wom - an

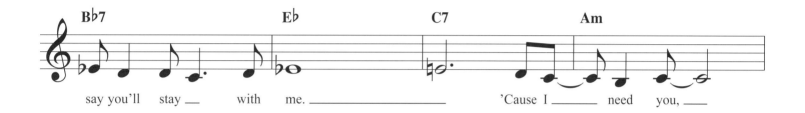

say you'll stay __ with me. _____ 'Cause I _____ need you, ___

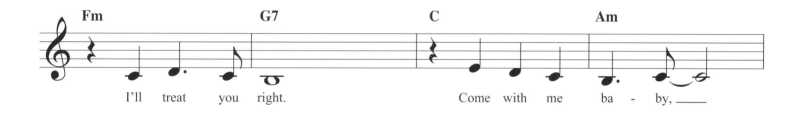

I'll treat you right. Come with me ba - by, ____

be mine to - night. _____

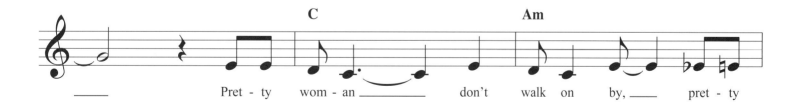

____ Pret - ty wom - an _____ don't walk on by, ___ pret - ty

wom - an _____ don't make me cry, ___ pret - ty wom - an _____

154

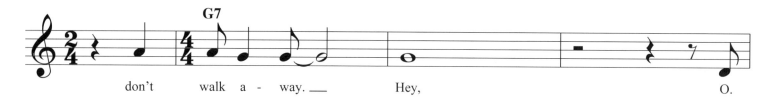

don't walk a - way. ___ Hey, O.

K. If that's the way it must be ___ O. K.

I guess I'll go on home, ___ it's late. ___ There'll be to -

mor - row night but wait! What do I see? _____

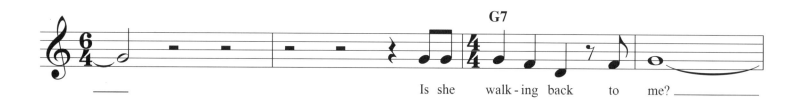

___ Is she walk - ing back to me? _____

___ Yeah, ___ she's walk - ing back to me! _____

___ Oh, _____ pret - ty wom - an.

ON GOLDEN POND
Main Theme from ON GOLDEN POND

Music by DAVE GRUSIN

OVER THE RAINBOW
from THE WIZARD OF OZ

Music by HAROLD ARLEN
Lyric by E.Y. "YIP" HARBURG

PUTTIN' ON THE RITZ
from the Motion Picture PUTTIN' ON THE RITZ

Words and Music by
IRVING BERLIN

Moderate Swing

If you're blue and you ___ don't know where to go to, why don't you go where fash - ion

sits, _____ put - tin' on the Ritz.

Dif - f'rent types who wear ___ a day coat, pants with stripes and cut - a - way coat, per - fect

fits, _____ put - tin' on the Ritz.

Stroll - ing up the av - e - nue so hap - py. ___
(Alt: Dressed up like a mil - lion dol - lar troup - er. ___

All dressed up just like an Eng - lish chap - pie, ___ ver - y snap - py.
Try - ing hard to look like Gar - y Coo - per, ___ su - per du - per.)

Come let's mix where Rock - e - fel - lers walk with sticks or "um - ber - el - las" in their

mitts, _____ put - tin' on the Ritz. _____

Ritz. _____

THE RAINBOW CONNECTION
from THE MUPPET MOVIE

Words and Music by PAUL WILLIAMS
and KENNETH L. ASCHER

Moderately, with a lilt

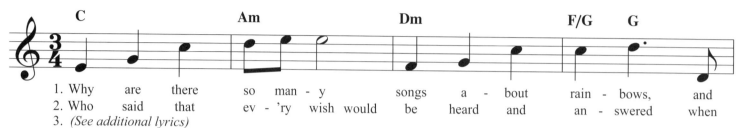

1. Why are there so man-y songs a-bout rain-bows, and
2. Who said that ev-'ry wish would be heard and an-swered when
3. *(See additional lyrics)*

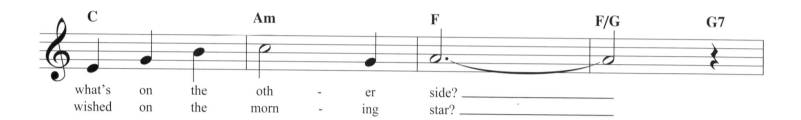

what's on the oth-er side? _____
wished on the morn-ing star? _____

Rain-bows are vi-sions, __ but on-ly il-lu-sions, and
Some-bod-y thought of that, and some-one be-lieved it;

rain-bows have noth-ing to hide. _____
look what it's done _____ so far. _____

So we've been told, and some choose to be-lieve it,
What's so a-maz-ing that keeps us star-gaz-ing, and

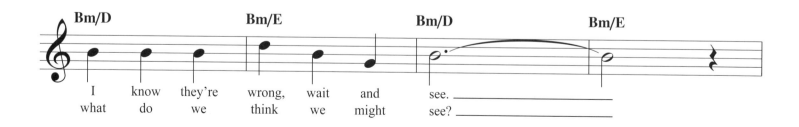

I know they're wrong, wait and see. _____
what do we think we might see? _____

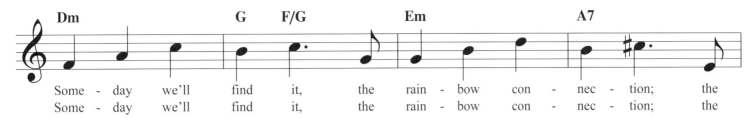

Some - day we'll find it, the rain - bow con - nec - tion; the
Some - day we'll find it, the rain - bow con - nec - tion; the

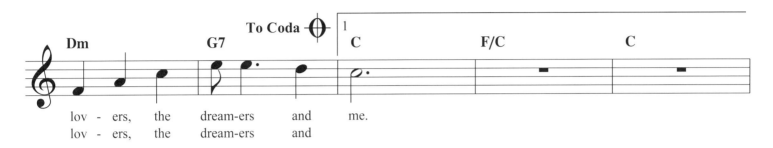

To Coda ⊕

lov - ers, the dream-ers and me.
lov - ers, the dream-ers and

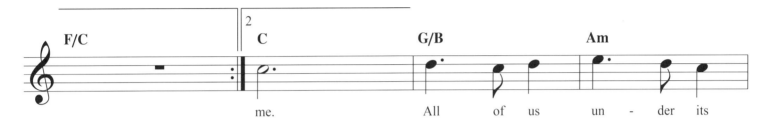

me. All of us un - der its

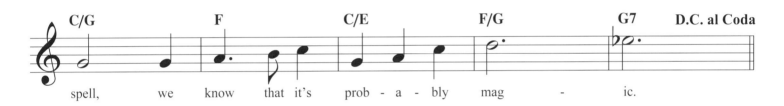

D.C. al Coda

spell, we know that it's prob - a - bly mag - ic.

CODA ⊕

me. La da da dee da da do la

la da da da dee da do. _____

Additional Lyrics

3. Have you been half asleep and have you heard voices?
   I've heard them calling my name.
   Is this the sweet sound that calls the young sailors?
   The voice might be one and the same.
   I've heard it too many times to ignore it.
   It's something that I'm s'posed to be.
   Someday we'll find it,
   The rainbow connection;
   The lovers, the dreamers and me.

RAINDROPS KEEP FALLIN' ON MY HEAD
from BUTCH CASSIDY AND THE SUNDANCE KID

Lyrics by HAL DAVID
Music by BURT BACHARACH

THE SHADOW OF YOUR SMILE
Love Theme from THE SANDPIPER

Music by JOHNNY MANDEL
Words by PAUL FRANCIS WEBSTER

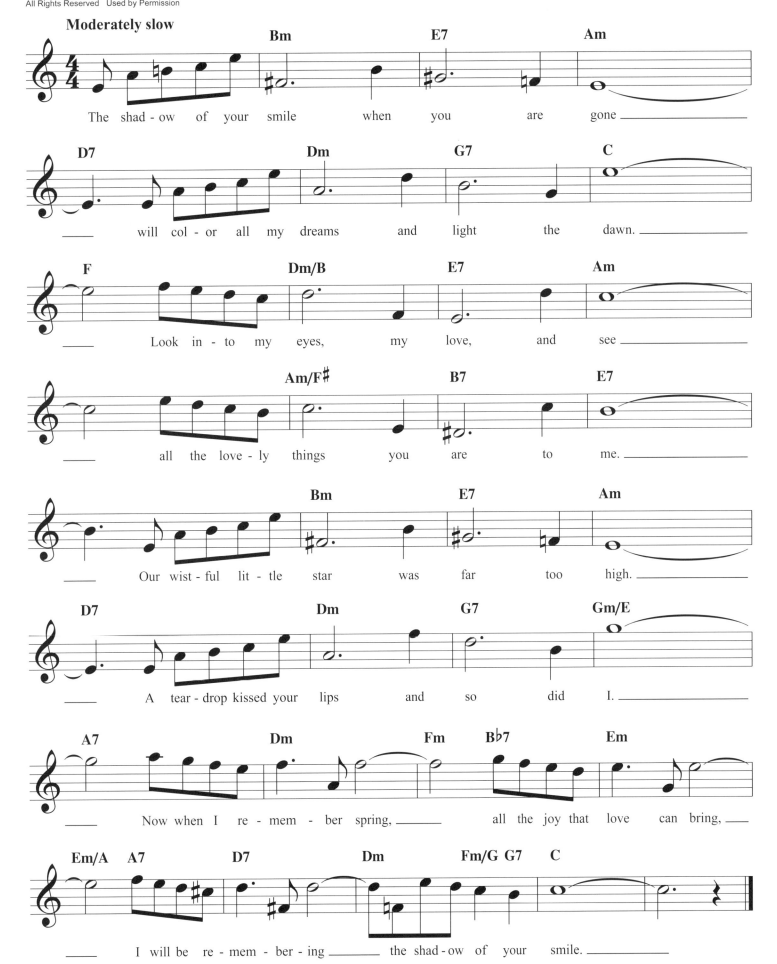

THE ROSE
from the Twentieth Century-Fox Motion Picture Release THE ROSE

Words and Music by
AMANDA McBROOM

Delicately

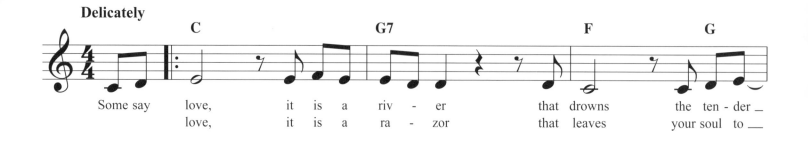

Some say love, it is a riv - er that drowns the ten - der _
love, it is a ra - zor that leaves your soul to _

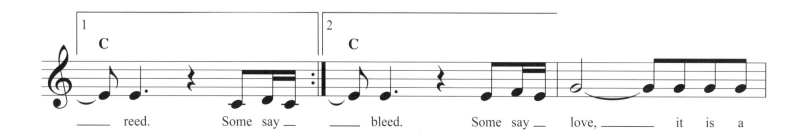

_ reed. Some say _ _ bleed. Some say _ love, _____ it is a

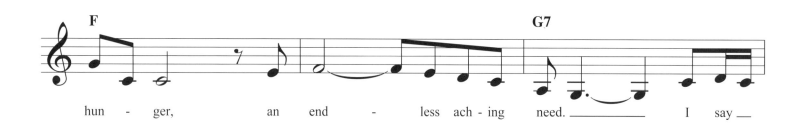

hun - ger, an end - less ach - ing need. _____ I say _

love, it is a flow - er, and you, its on - ly

seed. _____ It's the _ heart a - fraid of
night has been too

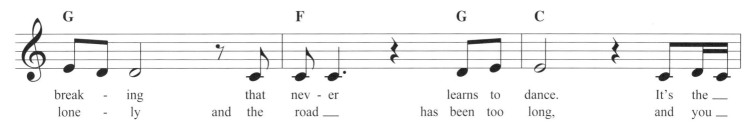

break - ing that nev - er learns to dance. It's the __
lone - ly and the road __ has been too long, and you __

dream _____ a - fraid of wak - ing that nev - er takes the __
think _____ that love is on - ly for the luck - y and the __

____ chance. It's the __ one _____ who won't be tak - en, who
____ strong, just re - mem - ber _____ in the win - ter far be -

can - not seem to give, __ and the __ soul a - fraid of
neath _____ the bit - ter snows _ lies the __ seed that with the

1
dy - in' that nev - er learns to live. _____
sun's __ love in the

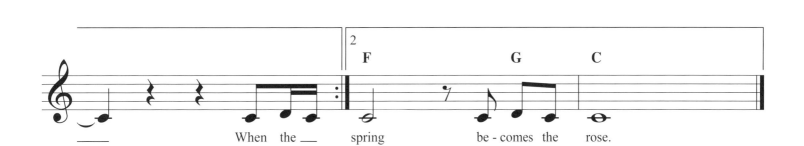

2
____ When the __ spring be - comes the rose.

LOVE THEME FROM "ST. ELMO'S FIRE"
from the Motion Picture ST. ELMO'S FIRE

Words and Music by
DAVID FOSTER

Moderately slow

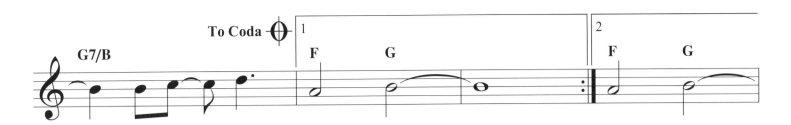

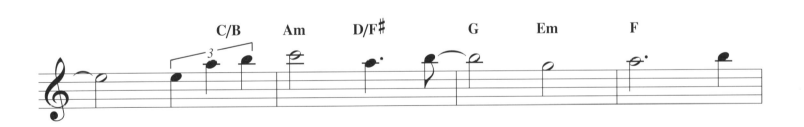

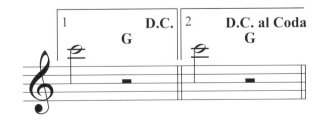

SHALLOW
from A STAR IS BORN

Words and Music by STEFANI GERMANOTTA,
MARK RONSON, ANDREW WYATT
and ANTHONY ROSSOMANDO

Moderately

Male: Tell me some-thing, girl: _____ are you hap-py in this
Female: Tell me some-thing, boy: _____ aren't you tired, __ tryin' to

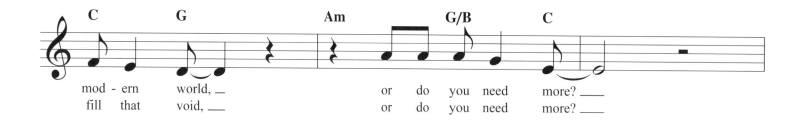

mod - ern world, _ or do you need more? _____
fill that void, _ or do you need more? _____

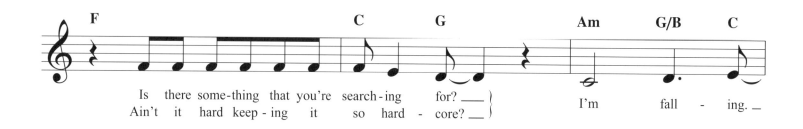

Is there some-thing that you're search-ing for? _____ }
Ain't it hard keep-ing it so hard - core? _____ }
I'm fall - ing.

_____ In all the good times I find my - self ___ long - ing _

_ for change, _ and in the bad times I

169

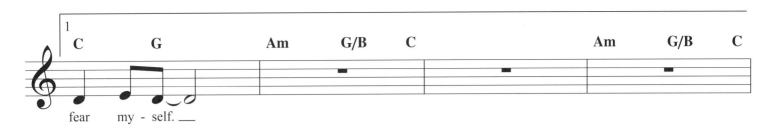

fear my - self. ___

fear my - self. ___ I'm off the deep ___ end.

Watch as I dive ___ in: I'll nev - er meet ___ the ground. ___

Crash through the sur - face, where they can't hurt ___ us. We're far from the shal - low now. ___

___ *Both:* In the shal, -al, shal, -al - low, ___

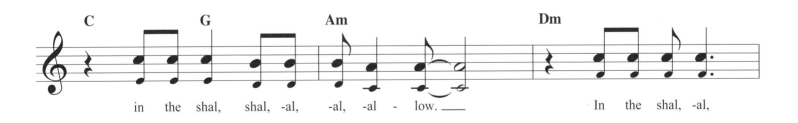

in the shal, shal, -al, -al, -al - low. ___ In the shal, -al,

shal, -al - low, ___ we're far from the shal - low now. ___

170

SOMEWHERE IN MY MEMORY
from the Twentieth Century Fox Motion Picture HOME ALONE

Words by LESLIE BRICUSSE
Music by JOHN WILLIAMS

Gently and with simplicity

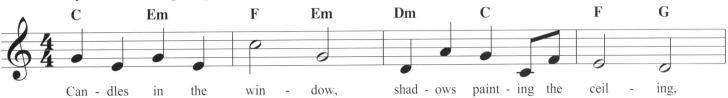

Can - dles in the win - dow, shad - ows paint - ing the ceil - ing,

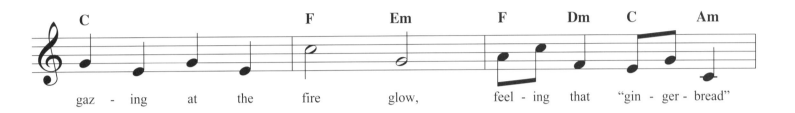

gaz - ing at the fire glow, feel - ing that "gin - ger - bread"

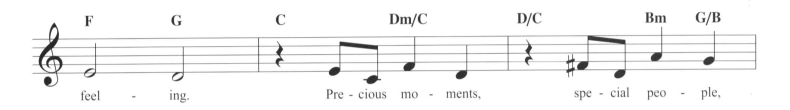

feel - ing. Pre - cious mo - ments, spe - cial peo - ple,

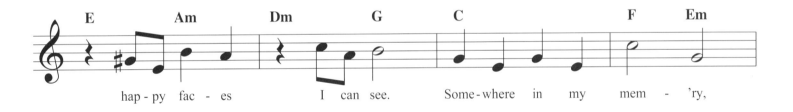

hap - py fac - es I can see. Some - where in my mem - 'ry,

Christ - mas joys all a - round me, liv - ing in my mem - 'ry,

all of the mu - sic, all of the mag - ic, all of the fam - 'ly

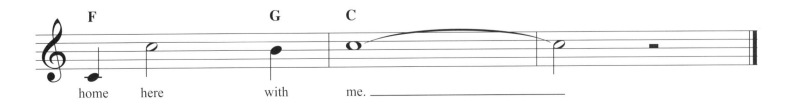

home here with me.

SINGIN' IN THE RAIN
from SINGIN' IN THE RAIN

Lyric by ARTHUR FREED
Music by NACIO HERB BROWN

I'm sing - in' in the rain,   just sing - in' in the

rain.   What a glo - ri - ous feel - ing! I'm hap - py a - gain.

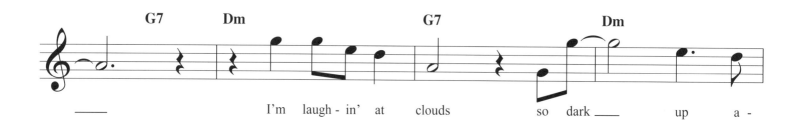

I'm laugh - in' at clouds   so dark ___ up a -

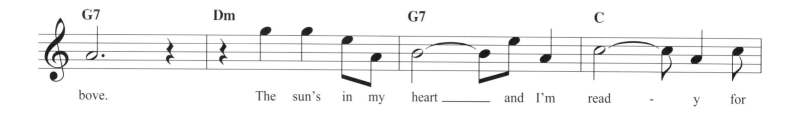

bove.   The sun's in my heart ___ and I'm read - y for

love.   Let the storm - y clouds chase ev - 'ry - one ___ from the place. ___

___   Come on ___ with the rain; ___   I've a smile ___ on my

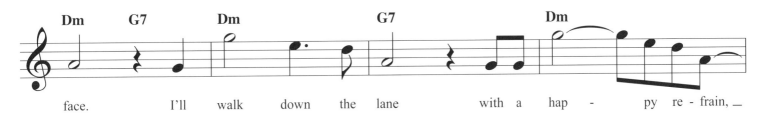

face. I'll walk down the lane with a hap - py re - frain, ___

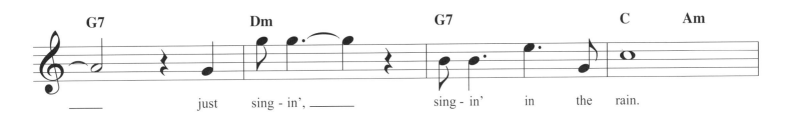

___ just sing - in', _____ sing - in' in the rain.

Danc - in' in the rain. Hey - yo - ya _____ ya - dia - da -

dia. *(Instrumental)* I'm hap - py a - gain. ___

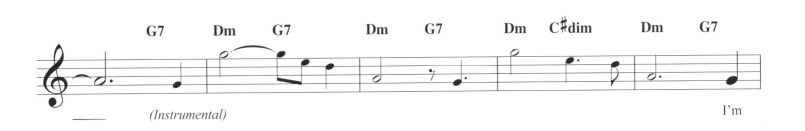

___ *(Instrumental)* I'm

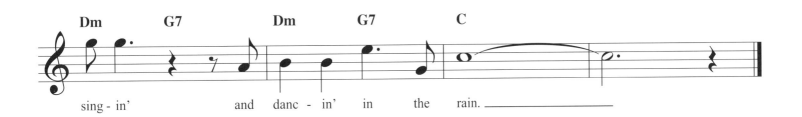

sing - in' and danc - in' in the rain. _____

SKYFALL
from the Motion Picture SKYFALL

Words and Music by ADELE ADKINS
and PAUL EPWORTH

Slow, mysterious

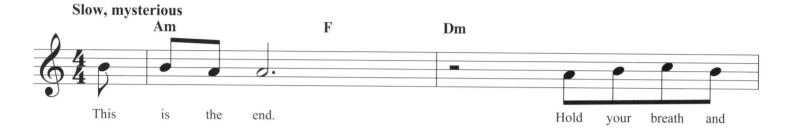

This is the end. Hold your breath and

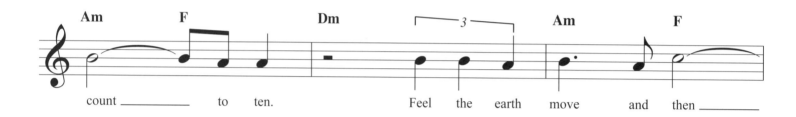

count to ten. Feel the earth move and then

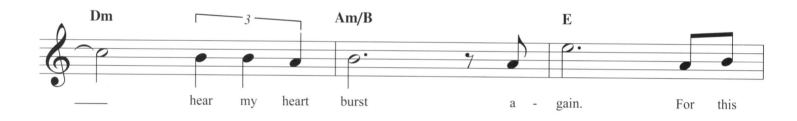

hear my heart burst a-gain. For this

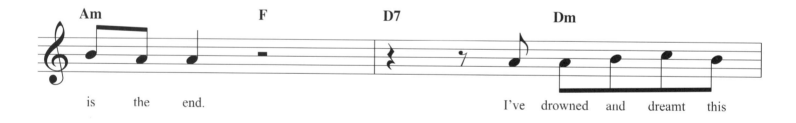

is the end. I've drowned and dreamt this

mo-ment. So o-ver-due I

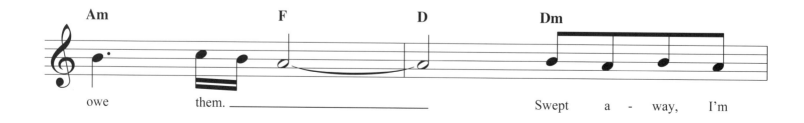

owe them. Swept a-way, I'm

175

sto - len.   Let the sky fall.   When it

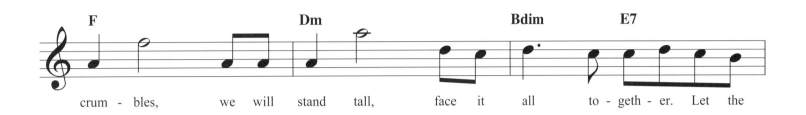

crum - bles,   we will stand tall,   face it all   to - geth - er.   Let the

sky   fall.   When it crum - bles,   we will stand tall,   face it

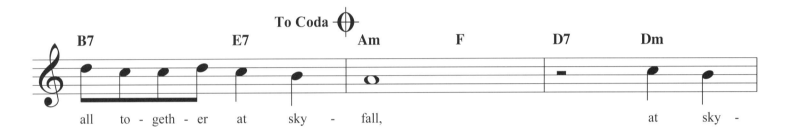

all   to - geth - er   at   sky - fall,   at   sky -

fall.   Sky - fall is   where we   start,

a   thou-sand miles and   poles a - part,   when worlds col - lide and

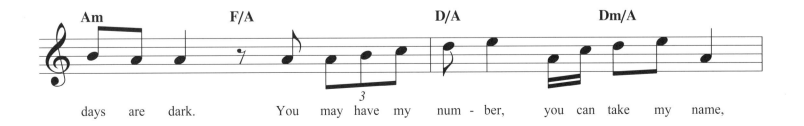

days   are   dark.   You   may have my   num - ber,   you can take   my name,

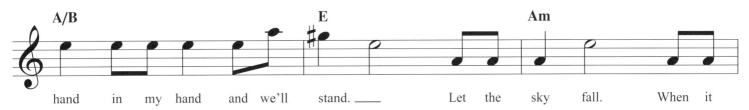

hand in my hand and we'll stand. ____ Let the sky fall. When it

crum - bles, we will stand tall, face it all to - geth - er. Let the

sky fall. When it crum - bles, we will stand tall, face it

all to - geth - er at sky - fall. Let the sky fall. _____

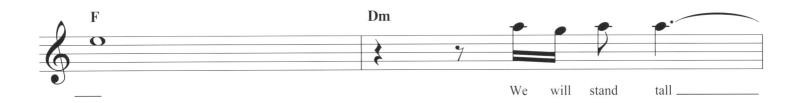

____ We will stand tall _____

_____ at sky - fall, _____

____ ooh. _____

SOMEWHERE IN TIME
from SOMEWHERE IN TIME

By JOHN BARRY

SOMEWHERE OUT THERE
from AN AMERICAN TAIL

Music by BARRY MANN and JAMES HORNER
Lyric by CYNTHIA WEIL

SOMEWHERE, MY LOVE
Lara's Theme from DOCTOR ZHIVAGO

Lyric by PAUL FRANCIS WEBSTER
Music by MAURICE JARRE

Moderately, with expression

Some - where, my love, there will be songs to sing,

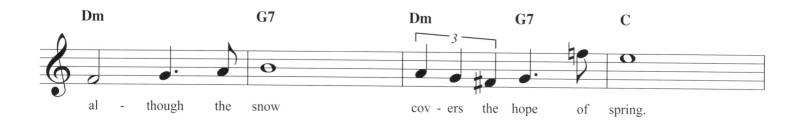

al - though the snow cov - ers the hope of spring.

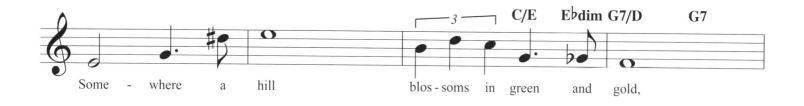

Some - where a hill blos - soms in green and gold,

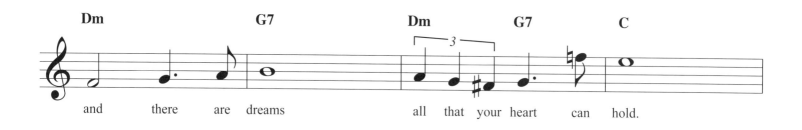

and there are dreams all that your heart can hold.

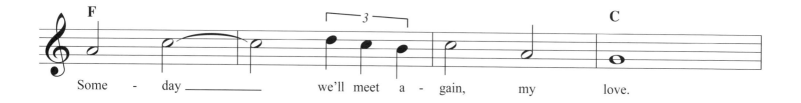

Some - day _____ we'll meet a - gain, my love.

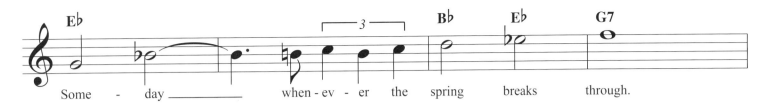

Some - day _____ when - ev - er the spring breaks through.

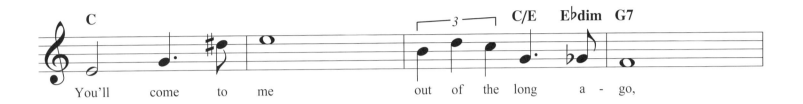

You'll come to me out of the long a - go,

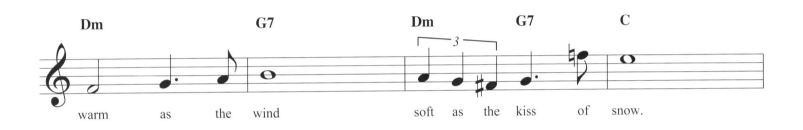

warm as the wind soft as the kiss of snow.

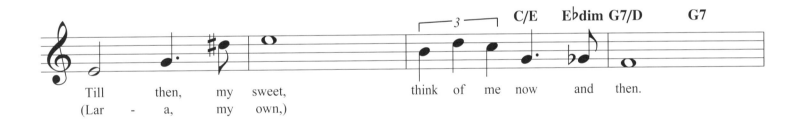

Till then, my sweet, think of me now and then.
(Lar - a, my own,)

God - speed, my love, 'til you are mine a - gain.

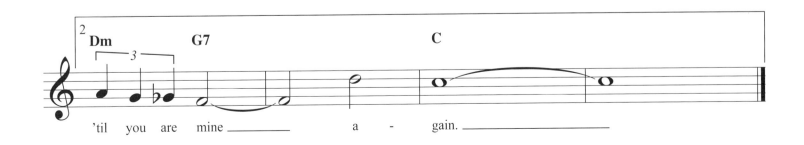

'til you are mine _____ a - gain. _____

SPEAK SOFTLY, LOVE
(Love Theme)
from the Paramount Picture THE GODFATHER

Words by LARRY KUSIK
Music by NINO ROTA

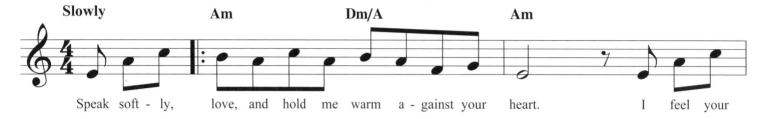

Speak soft - ly, love, and hold me warm a - gainst your heart. I feel your

words, the ten - der, trem - bling mo - ments start. We're in a world _____ our ver - y

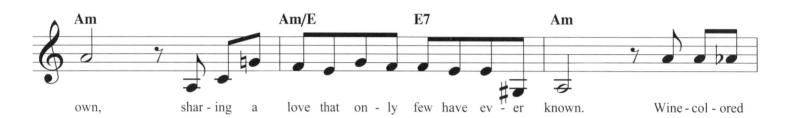

own, shar - ing a love that on - ly few have ev - er known. Wine - col - ored

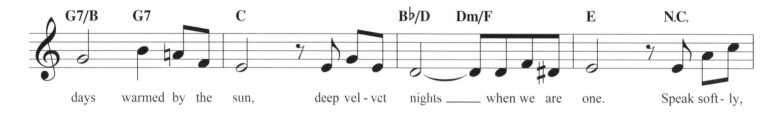

days warmed by the sun, deep vel - vet nights _____ when we are one. Speak soft - ly,

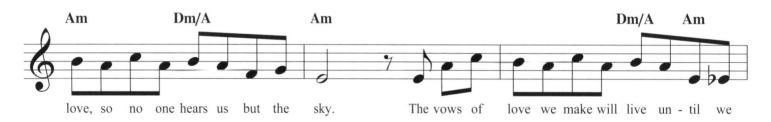

love, so no one hears us but the sky. The vows of love we make will live un - til we

die. My life is yours _____ and all be - cause you came in -

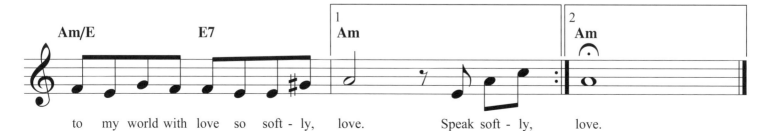

to my world with love so soft - ly, love. Speak soft - ly, love.

STAR TREK® THE MOTION PICTURE
Theme from the Paramount Picture STAR TREK: THE MOTION PICTURE

Music by JERRY GOLDSMITH

STAYIN' ALIVE
from the Motion Picture SATURDAY NIGHT FEVER

Words and Music by BARRY GIBB,
ROBIN GIBB and MAURICE GIBB

Well, you can tell ___ by the way I use ___ my walk, ___ I'm a wom-
___ get ___ low and I ___ get high ___ and if I ___

-an's man: no time to talk. ___
___ can't get ei - ther, I real - ly try. Got the

Mu - sic loud ___ and wom - en warm, ___ I've been
wings of heav - en on ___ my shoes, ___ I'm a

kicked a - round ___ since I ___ was born. ___ And now it's
danc - in' man ___ and I just can't lose. ___ You know it's

all right. ___ It's O. K. ___ And you may look ___ the oth - er way. ___
all right. ___ It's O. K. ___ I'll live to see ___ an - oth - er day. ___

We can try ___ to un-der-stand ___ the New York Times' ___ ef-fect ___ on man. ___

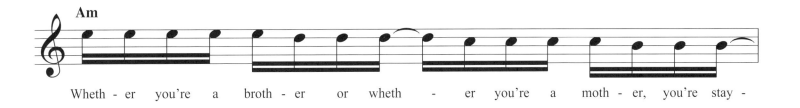

Am

Wheth - er you're a broth - er or wheth - er you're a moth - er, you're stay -

- in' a - live, ___ stay - in' a - live. ___

Feel the cit - y break - in' and ev - 'ry - bod - y shak - in' and we're

stay - in' a - live, ___ stay - in' a - live. ___ Ah, ha, ha, ha,

stay - in' a - live, ___ stay - in' a - live. ___ Ah, ha, ha, ha,

stay-in' a - live. _____

Well now, I ____

Life go - in' no - where. _____ Some - bod - y help me. _____

Some - bod - y help ___ me, yeah. _____

Life go - in' no - where. _____ Some - bod - y help ___ me, yeah. ___

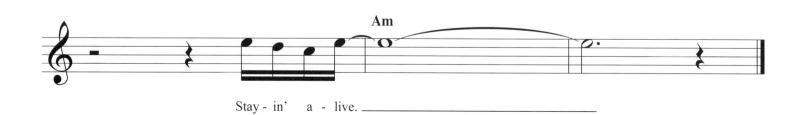

Stay - in' a - live. _____

SUMMER NIGHTS
from GREASE

Lyric and Music by WARREN CASEY
and JIM JACOBS

Moderately

Boy: "Sum-mer lov-in,' had me a blast." _____ Girl: "Sum-mer lov-in'
"She swam by me; she got a cramp." ___ "He ran by me;
"Took her bowl-ing in the ar-cade." _____ "We went stroll-ing;

hap-pened so fast." _____ Boy: "Met a girl, cra-zy for me." _____
got my suit damp." _____ "Saved her life; she near-ly drowned." _
drank lem-on-ade." _____ "We made out un-der the dock." _____

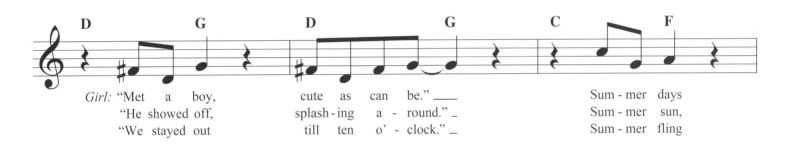

Girl: "Met a boy, cute as can be." ___ Sum-mer days
"He showed off, splash-ing a-round." _ Sum-mer sun,
"We stayed out till ten o'-clock." _ Sum-mer fling

1, 2

drift-ing a-way __ to, ___ uh, oh, those sum-mer nights. ___ Well-a, well-a, well-a
some-thing's be-gun. ___ But, __ uh, oh, those sum-mer nights. ___ Well-a, well-a, well-a
don't mean a thing. _ But, ___

uh. Tell me more. Tell me more. Did you get ver-y far? _____ Tell me more. Tell me
uh. Tell me more. Tell me more. Was it love at first sight? _____ Tell me more. Tell me

boy and girl meet. ___ But, ___ uh, oh those sum - mer nights. ___

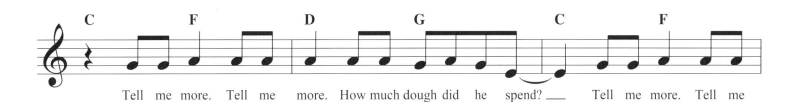

Tell me more. Tell me more. How much dough did he spend? ___ Tell me more. Tell me

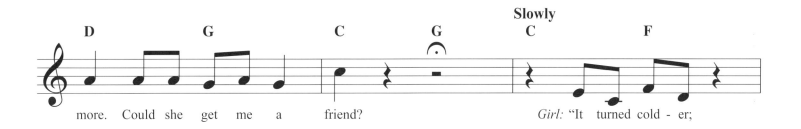

more. Could she get me a friend? *Girl:* "It turned cold - er;

that's where it ends." ___ *Boy:* "So I told her we'd still be friends." _

Girl: "Then we made our true love vow." ___ *Boy:* "Won - der what

she's do - in' now." _ Sum - mer dreams ripped at the seams. But, ___

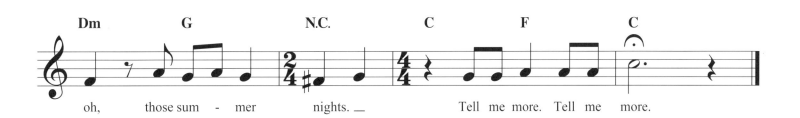

oh, those sum - mer nights. ___ Tell me more. Tell me more.

TAKE MY BREATH AWAY
(Love Theme)
from the Paramount Picture TOP GUN

Words and Music by GIORGIO MORODER
and TOM WHITLOCK

Moderately slow

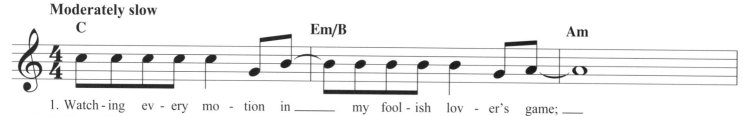

1. Watch-ing ev-ery mo-tion in _____ my fool-ish lov-er's game; _____
2., 3. (See additional lyrics)

(Instrumental)   on this end-less o-cean, fi - n'lly lov-ers know no shame. _____

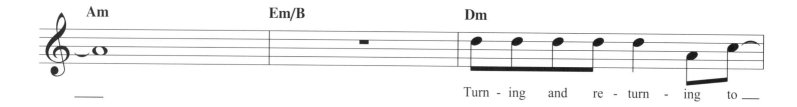

Turn - ing   and   re - turn - ing   to _____

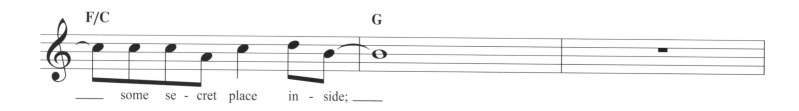

_____ some se-cret place in - side; _____

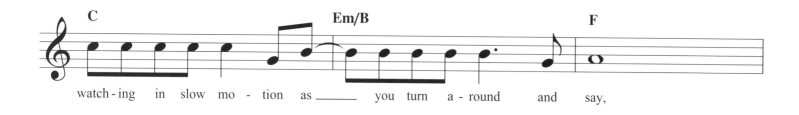

watch-ing   in   slow   mo - tion   as _____   you   turn   a - round   and   say,

"Take   my   breath   a - way."   _____   (Instrumental)

"Take my breath a - way." _____ *(Instrumental)*

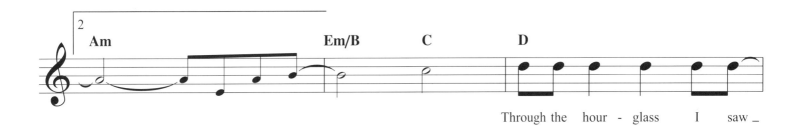

Through the hour - glass I saw _

____ you. In time ____ you slipped a - way. ____

When the mir - ror crashed, I called ____ you and turned ____ to hear you

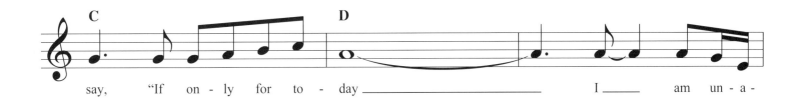

say, "If on - ly for to - day _____ I ____ am un - a -

192

fraid. _____ Take my breath a - way." _____ (Instrumental)

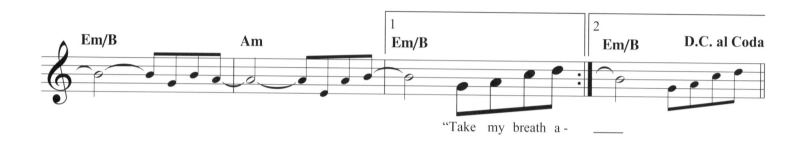

"Take my breath a - ___

CODA

_____ My love, ___ take my breath a - way. _____ (Instrumental)

My love, ___ take my breath a -

Additional Lyrics

2. Watching, I keep waiting, still anticipating love,
Never hesitating to become the fated ones.
Turning and returning to some secret place to hide;
Watching in slow motion as you turn to me and say,
"Take my breath away."
(To Bridge)

3. Watching every motion in this foolish lover's game;
Haunted by the notion somewhere there's a love in flames.
Turning and returning to some secret place inside;
Watching in slow motion as you turn my way and say,
"Take my breath away."
(To Coda)

THIS IS ME
from THE GREATEST SHOWMAN

Words and Music by BENJ PASEK
and JUSTIN PAUL

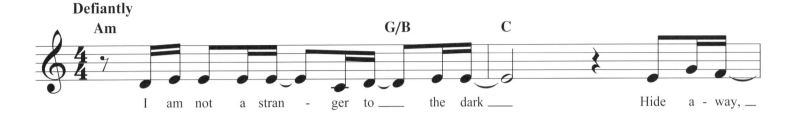

I am not a stran - ger to ___ the dark ___ Hide a - way, ___

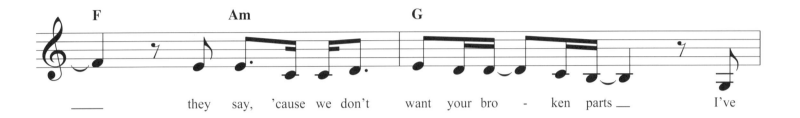

___ they say, 'cause we don't want your bro - ken parts ___ I've

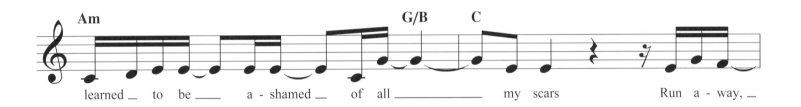

learned ___ to be ___ a - shamed ___ of all ___ my scars Run a - way, ___

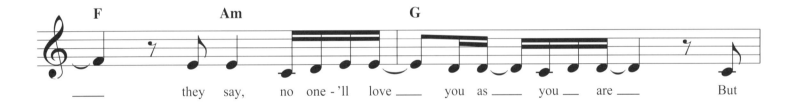

___ they say, no one -'ll love ___ you as ___ you ___ are ___ But

I won't let them break me down ___ to dust I know that there's a place ___ for us, ___

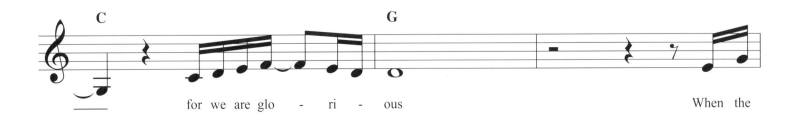

___ for we are glo - ri - ous When the

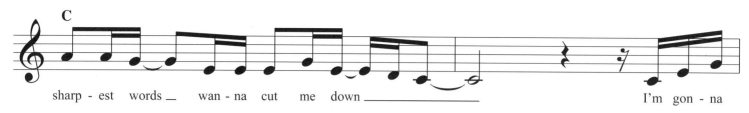

sharp - est words __ wan - na cut me down _____ I'm gon - na

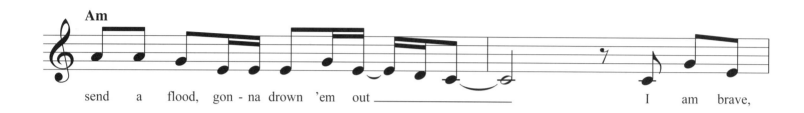

send a flood, gon - na drown 'em out _____ I am brave,

I am bruised, I am who ____ I'm meant __ to be This is me

Look out, __ 'cause here __ I come _____ and I'm march -

- in' on to the beat I drum _____ I'm not scared

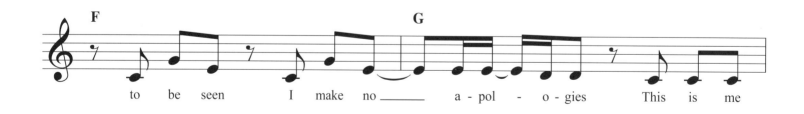

to be seen I make no _____ a - pol - o - gies This is me

Oh _____ Oh _____ Oh _____

Oh _____ Oh _____ Oh _____ oh, oh An -

oth - er round of bul - lets hits my skin Well, fi - re a - way, ____ 'cause to - day I won't let ___

____ the shame ___ sink ___ in ____ We are burst - in' through the bar - ri - cades ___ and

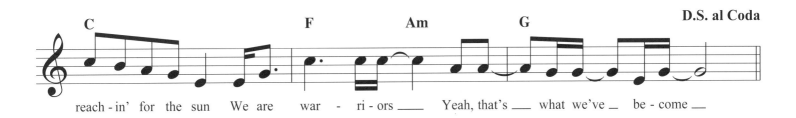

reach - in' for the sun We are war - ri - ors ____ Yeah, that's ___ what we've ___ be - come ___

oh, oh This is me Oh _____

Oh _____ Oh _____ Oh _____

Oh _____ Oh _____ oh, oh This is me

THAT'S AMORÉ
(That's Love)
from the Paramount Picture THE CADDY

Words by JACK BROOKS
Music by HARRY WARREN

Moderately

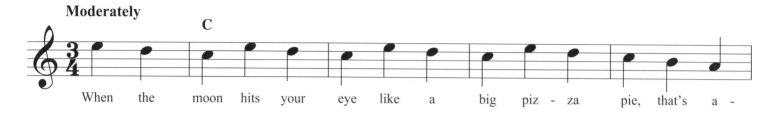

When the moon hits your eye like a big piz-za pie, that's a-

mor - é. _____ When the world seems to

shine like you've had too much wine, that's a - mor - é. _____

_____ Bells will ring, ting - a - ling - a - ling, ting - a - ling - a -

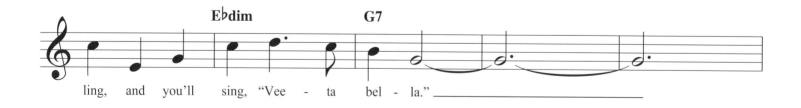

ling, and you'll sing, "Vee - ta bel - la." _____

Hearts will play, tip - py - tip - py - tay, tip - py - tip - py - tay like a

197

A TIME FOR US
(Love Theme)
from the Paramount Picture ROMEO AND JULIET

Words by LARRY KUSIK and EDDIE SNYDER
Music by NINO ROTA

Slowly and expressively

(I've Had)
THE TIME OF MY LIFE
from DIRTY DANCING

Words and Music by FRANKE PREVITE,
JOHN DeNICOLA and DONALD MARKOWITZ

1. I've been wait-ing for so long, _____ now I've fi-n'lly found some-one ___ to stand by
2. (See additional lyrics)

me. _____ We saw the writ-ing on the wall _____ as we

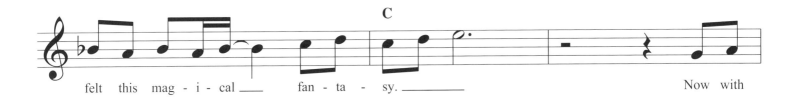

felt this mag-i-cal ___ fan-ta-sy. _____ Now with

Omit these measures 2nd time

pas-sion in our eyes _____ there's no way we could dis-guise _____ it se-cret-

ly. _____ So we take each oth-er's hand, _____ 'cause we

200

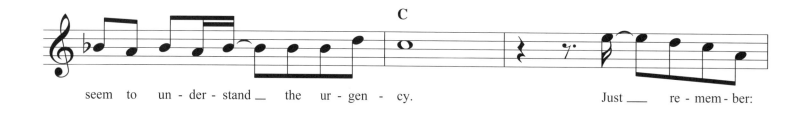

seem to un-der-stand __ the ur-gen-cy.   Just __ re-mem-ber:

Bridge

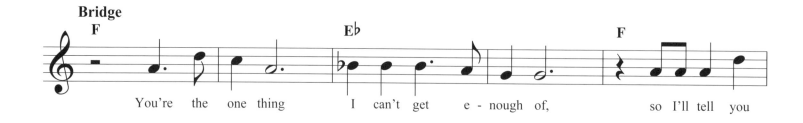

You're the one thing   I can't get e-nough of,   so I'll tell you

some-thing,   this could be love.   Be-cause   I've   had   the time of my
                                                        I've   had   the time of my

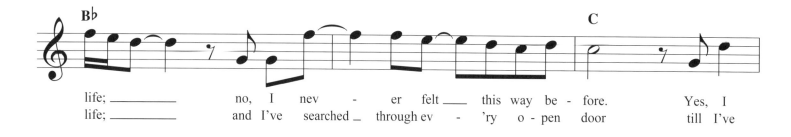

life; _____   no, I nev - er felt __ this way be - fore.   Yes, I
life; _____   and I've searched __ through ev - 'ry o - pen door   till I've

swear   it's the truth, _____   and I owe it all to you. __
found   the truth, _____

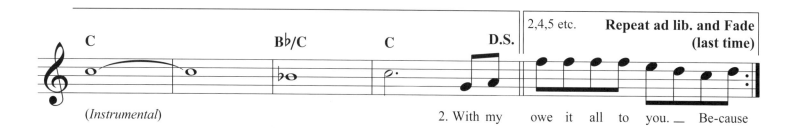

(*Instrumental*)   2. With my owe it all to you. __ Be-cause

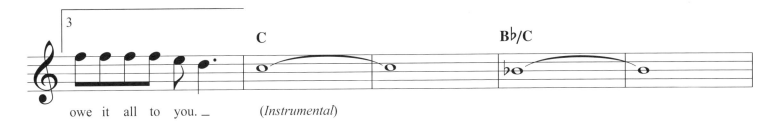

owe it all to you. ___ (*Instrumental*)

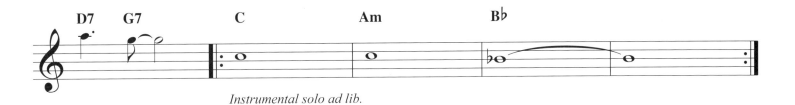

Instrumental solo ad lib.

Solo ends I've had the time of my

life, _____ and I nev-er felt ___ this way be-fore. Yes, I

swear it's the truth _____ and I owe it all to you. ___

Additional Lyrics

2. With my body and soul
I want you more and more than you'll ever know.
So we'll just let it go,
Don't be afraid to lose control.
Yes, I know what's on your mind
When you say "Stay with me tonight."
Just remember…
Bridge

TIME WARP
from THE ROCKY HORROR PICTURE SHOW

Words and Music by
RICHARD O'BRIEN

Medium Rock beat

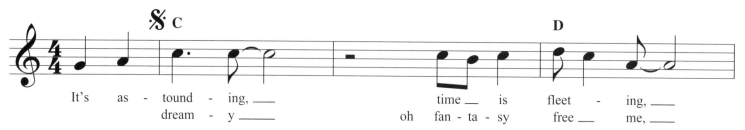

It's as- tound - ing, ___ time ___ is fleet - ing, ___
dream - y ___ oh fan- ta- sy free ___ me, ___

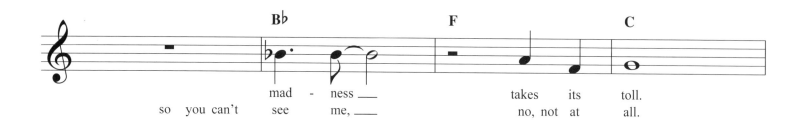

mad - ness ___ takes its toll.
so you can't see me, ___ no, not at all.

But lis - ten close - ly ___ not for ver - y much long -
In an- oth- er di - men - sion ___ with voy- eur- is- tic in- ten -

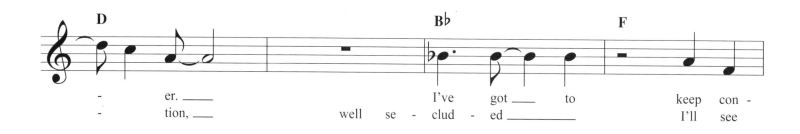

- er. ___ I've got ___ to keep con -
- tion, ___ well se - clud - ed ___ I'll see

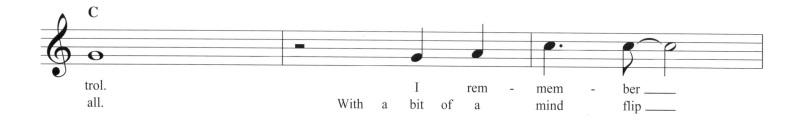

trol.
all.   I re- mem - ber ___
With a bit of a mind flip ___

do-ing the time _____ warp, _____ drink - ing _____
you're in - to the time _____ slip, _____ noth - ing _____

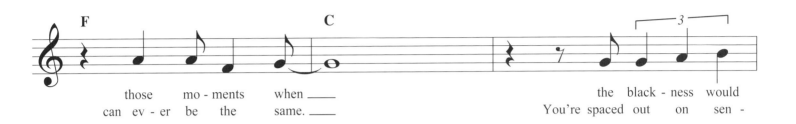

those mo - ments when _____ the black - ness would
can ev - er be the same. _____ You're spaced out on sen -

hit me _____ and the void would be call - ing. _____)
sa - tion _____ like you're un - der se - da - tion. _____)

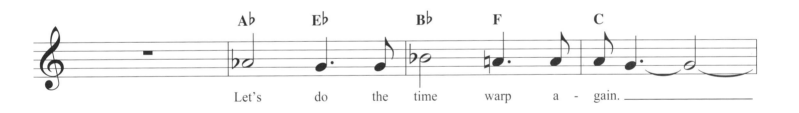

Let's do the time warp a - gain. _____

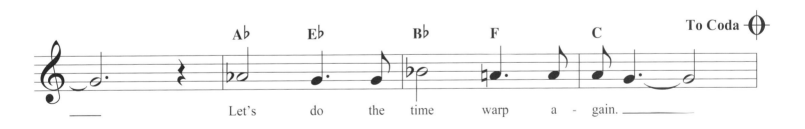

_____ Let's do the time warp a - gain. _____

It's just a jump to the left _____ and then a step to the ri -

-i-i-i-i-i-ight.   With your hands on your hips, ____

you bring your knees in tight. ____   But it's the pel - vic

thrust ____   that real - ly drives you in - sa - a - a - a - a - ane. _

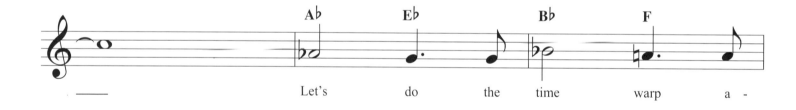

____   Let's do the time warp a -

gain. ____   Let's do the time warp a -

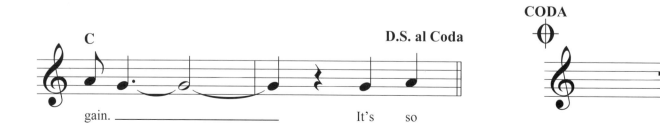

gain. ____   It's so

A WHOLE NEW WORLD
from ALADDIN

Music by ALAN MENKEN
Lyrics by TIM RICE

UNCHAINED MELODY
from the Motion Picture UNCHAINED

Lyric by HY ZARET
Music by ALEX NORTH

Flowing

Oh, my love, my dar - ling, I've hun - gered for your

touch a long, lone - ly time. _____

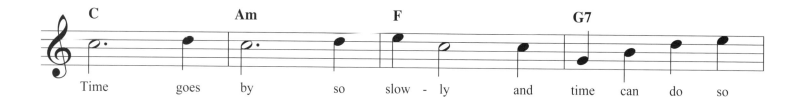

Time goes by so slow - ly and time can do so

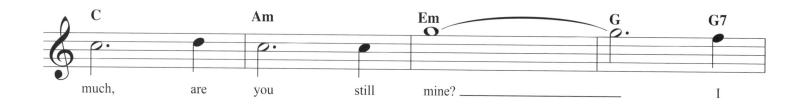

much, are you still mine? _____

I

need   your   love, _____   I   need   your   love, _____   God

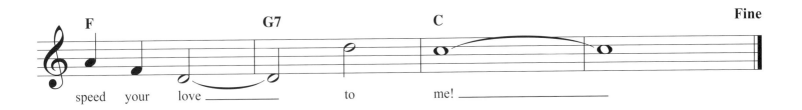

Fine

speed   your   love _____   to   me! _____

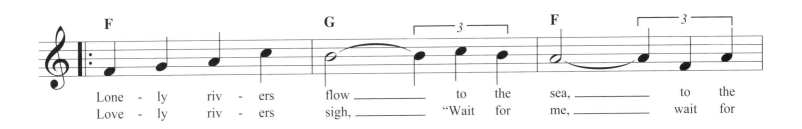

Lone - ly   riv - ers   flow _____   to   the   sea, _____   to   the
Love - ly   riv - ers   sigh, _____   "Wait   for   me, _____   wait   for

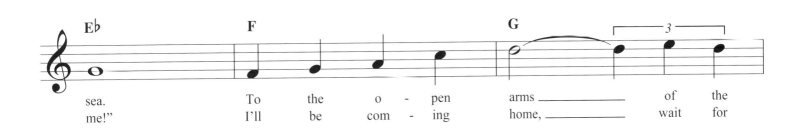

sea.   To   the   o - pen   arms _____   of   the
me!"   I'll   be   com - ing   home, _____   wait   for

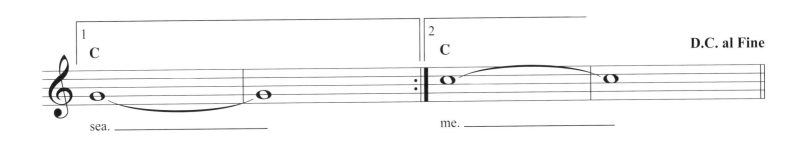

1.   C
sea. _____

2.   C
me. _____

D.C. al Fine

UP WHERE WE BELONG
from the Paramount Picture AN OFFICER AND A GENTLEMAN

Words by WILL JENNINGS
Music by BUFFY SAINTE-MARIE and JACK NITZSCHE

THE WAY WE WERE

from the Motion Picture THE WAY WE WERE

Words by ALAN and MARILYN BERGMAN
Music by MARVIN HAMLISCH

Slowly

Mem - 'ries _____ light the cor - ners of my mind.
pic - tures _____ of the smiles we left be - hind,

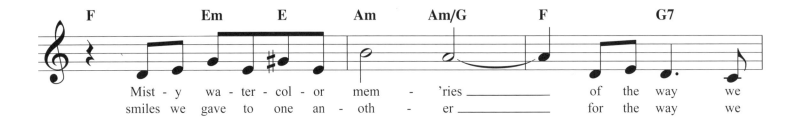

Mist - y wa - ter - col - or mem - 'ries _____ of the way we
smiles we gave to one an - oth - er _____ for the way we

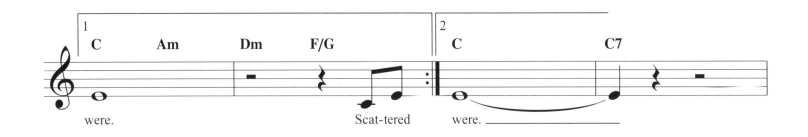

were.   Scat-tered
were. _____

Can it be that it was all so sim - ple then, or has time re - writ - ten ev - 'ry

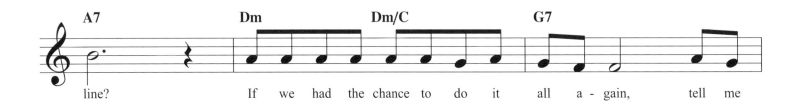

line?   If we had the chance to do it all a - gain, tell me

211

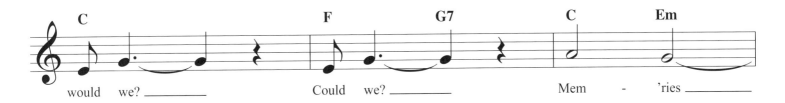

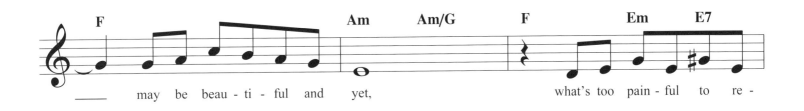

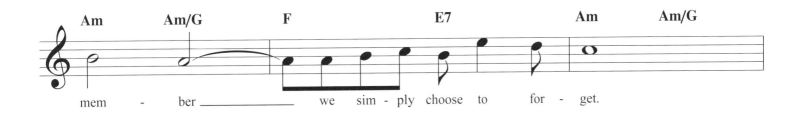

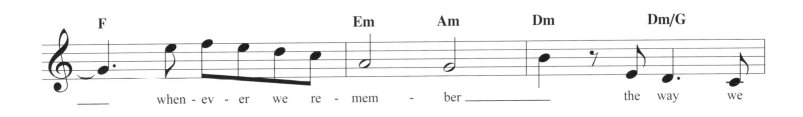

WHAT A WONDERFUL WORLD
featured in the Motion Picture GOOD MORNING VIETNAM

Words and Music by GEORGE DAVID WEISS
and BOB THIELE

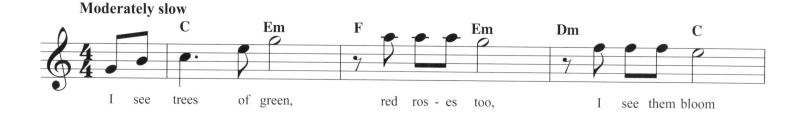

I see trees of green, red ros-es too, I see them bloom

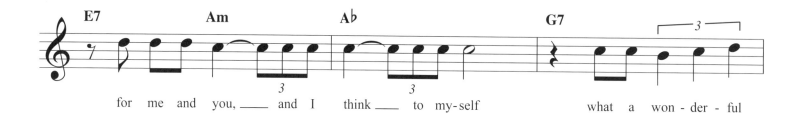

for me and you, ___ and I think ___ to my-self what a won-der-ful

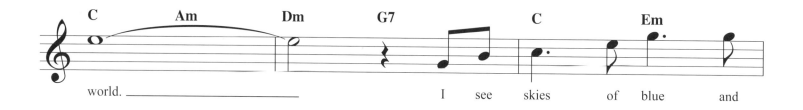

world. ___ I see skies of blue and

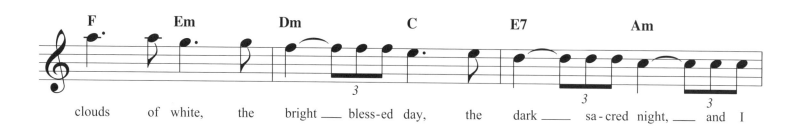

clouds of white, the bright ___ bless-ed day, the dark ___ sa-cred night, ___ and I

think ___ to my-self what a won-der-ful world. ___

The col-ors of the rain-bow, so pret-ty in the sky are

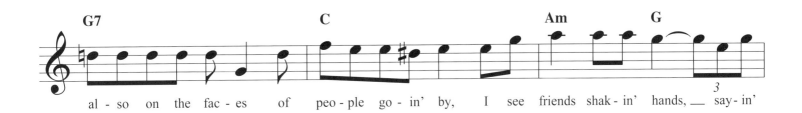

al - so on the fac-es of peo-ple go-in' by, I see friends shak-in' hands, ___ say-in'

"How do you do?" They're real - ly say - in' "I love you." I hear

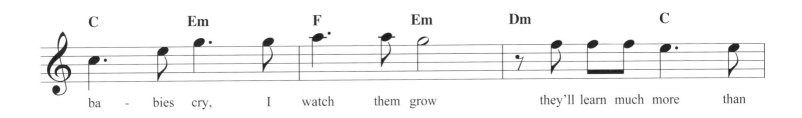

ba - bies cry, I watch them grow they'll learn much more than

I'll ___ ev - er know ___ and I think ___ to my-self what a won - der - ful

world. _____ Yes, I think to my - self

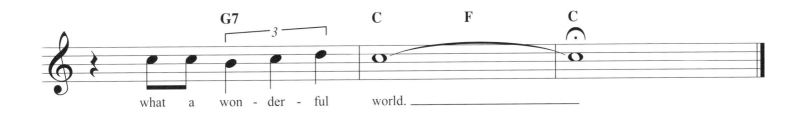

what a won - der - ful world. _____

WHEN I FALL IN LOVE
featured in the TriStar Motion Picture SLEEPLESS IN SEATTLE

Words by EDWARD HEYMAN
Music by VICTOR YOUNG

Slowly. with feeling

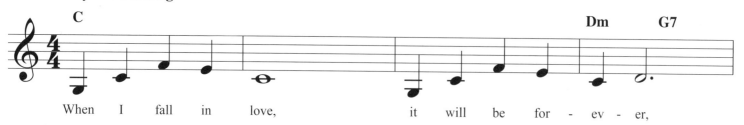

When I fall in love, it will be for - ev - er,

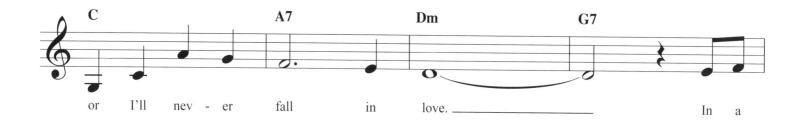

or I'll nev - er fall in love. _____ In a

rest - less world like this is, love is end - ed be - fore it's be -

gun. And too man - y moon - light kiss - es seem to

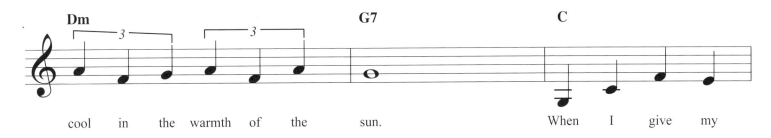

cool in the warmth of the sun. When I give my

heart, it will be com - plete - ly, or I'll nev - er

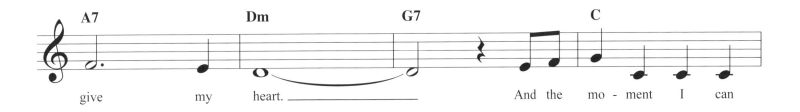

give my heart. And the mo - ment I can

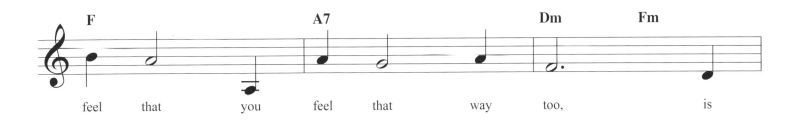

feel that you feel that way too, is

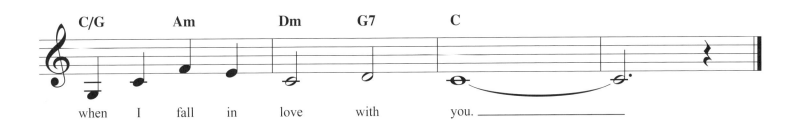

when I fall in love with you.

WHERE DO I BEGIN
(Love Theme)
from the Paramount Picture LOVE STORY

Words by CARL SIGMAN
Music by FRANCIS LAI

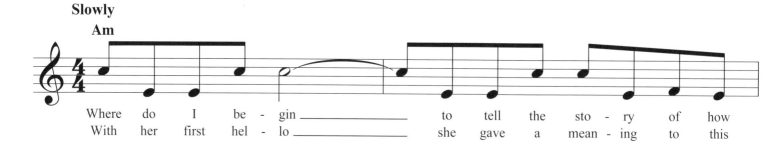

Where do I be-gin _____ to tell the sto-ry of how
With her first hel-lo _____ she gave a mean-ing to this

great a love can be, _____ The sweet love sto-ry that is
emp-ty world of mine; _____ There'll nev-er be an-oth-er

old-er than the sea, The sim-ple truth a-bout the
love, an-oth-er time; She came in-to my life and

love she brings to me? _____ Where do I start?
made the liv-ing fine. _____

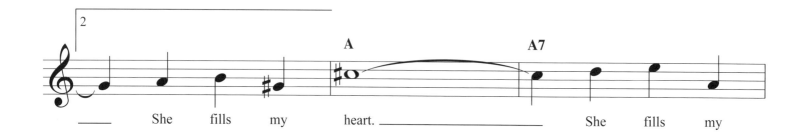

_____ She fills my heart. _____ She fills my

heart _____ with ver - y spe - cial things, __ with an - gel songs, _____ with wild i -

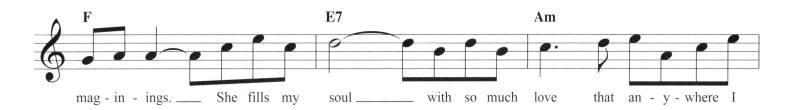

mag - in - ings. ___ She fills my soul _____ with so much love that an - y - where I

go _____ I'm nev - er lone - ly. _____ With her a - long, _____ who could be

lone - ly? _____ I reach for her hand, _____ it's al - ways there. _____

How long does it last? _____ Can love be meas - ured by the hours __ in a day? _____

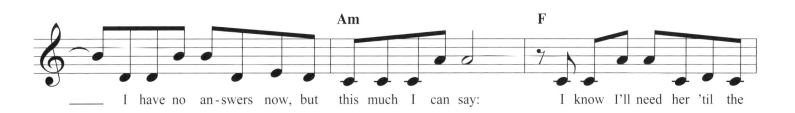

_____ I have no an - swers now, but this much I can say: I know I'll need her 'til the

stars all burn a - way. _____ and she'll be there. _____

THE WIND BENEATH MY WINGS
from the Original Motion Picture BEACHES

Words and Music by LARRY HENLEY
and JEFF SILBAR

Slowly flowing, in 2

1. It must have been cold ____ there in my shad - ow,
2., 3. *See additional lyrics*

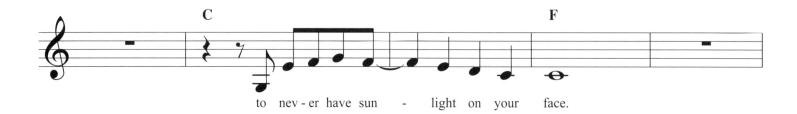

to nev - er have sun - light on your face.

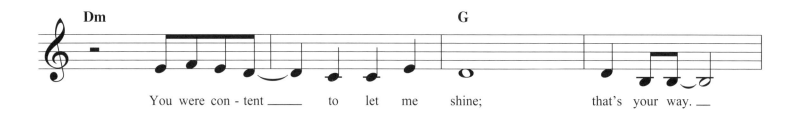

You were con - tent ____ to let me shine; that's your way. ____

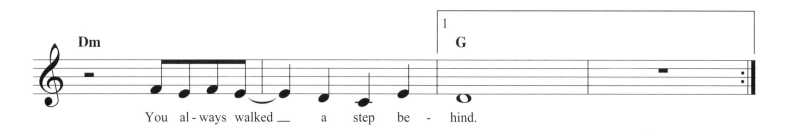

You al - ways walked ____ a step be - hind.

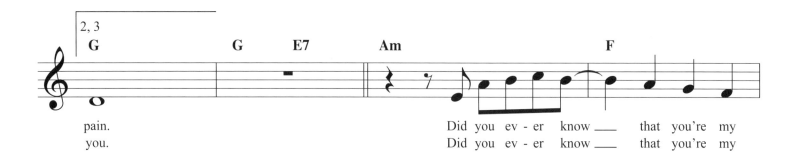

pain.
you.

Did you ev - er know ____ that you're my
Did you ev - er know ____ that you're my

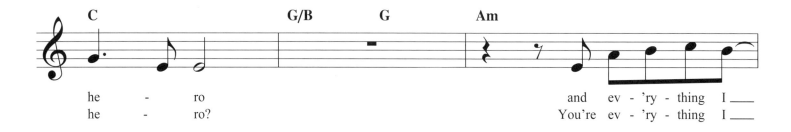

he - ro
he - ro?

and ev - 'ry - thing I ____
You're ev - 'ry - thing I ____

219

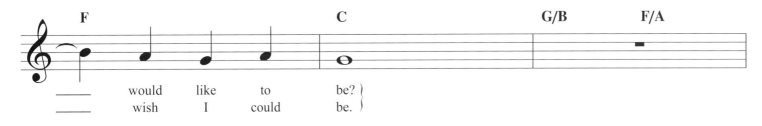

would like to be?
wish I could be.

I can fly high - er than an ea - gle, _____

To Coda

_____ for you are the wind _____ be - neath my

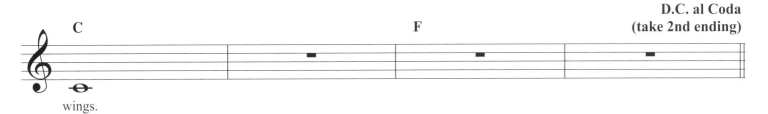

D.C. al Coda
(take 2nd ending)

wings.

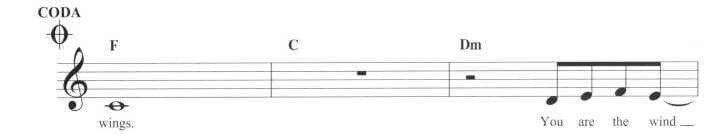

CODA

wings.   You are the wind _

_____ be - neath my wings. _____

Additional Lyrics

2. So I was the one with all the glory,
   While you were the one with all the strength.
   A beautiful face without a name for so long,
   A beautiful smile to hide the pain.

3. It might have appeared to go unnoticed,
   But I've got it all here in my heart.
   I want you to know I know the truth, of course I know it.
   I would be nothing without you.

THE WINDMILLS OF YOUR MIND
Theme from THE THOMAS CROWN AFFAIR

Words by ALAN and MARILYN BERGMAN
Music by MICHEL LEGRAND

Round like a cir-cle in a spi-ral, like a wheel with-in a wheel, Nev-er end-ing or be-
mind! Like a tun-nel that you fol-low to a tun-nel of its own, Down a hol-low to a

gin-ning on an ev-er spin-ning reel. Like a snow-ball down a moun-tain, or a car-ni-val bal-
cav-ern where the sun has nev-er shone. Like a door that keeps re-volv-ing in a half for-got-ten

loon, Like a car-ou-sel that's turn-ing, run-ning rings a-round the moon. } Like a clock whose hands are
dream, Or the rip-ples from a peb-ble some-one toss-es in a stream. }

sweep-ing past the min-utes of its face, And the world is like an ap-ple whirl-ing si-lent-ly in

space, Like the cir-cles that you find in the wind-mills of your mind! Keys that jin-gle in your

pock-et, words that jan-gle in your head. Why did sum-mer go so quick-ly? Was it some-thing that you

221

said? Lov-ers walk a-long a shore and leave their foot-prints in the sand. Is the sound of dis-tant

drum-ming just the fin-gers of your hand? Pic-tures hang-ing in a hall-way and the frag-ment of a

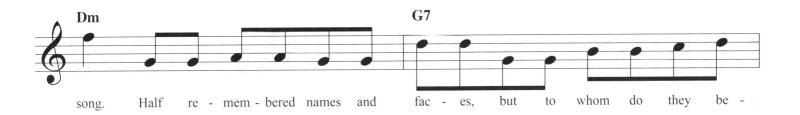

song. Half re-mem-bered names and fac-es, but to whom do they be-

long? When you knew that it was o-ver, you were sud-den-ly a-ware That the au-tumn leaves were
(*Girl:* When you knew that it was o-ver in the au-tumn of good-byes, For a mo-ment you could

turn-ing to the col-or of her hair! Like a cir-cle in a spi-ral, like a wheel with-in a
not re-call the col-or of his eyes!)

wheel, Nev-er end-ing or be-gin-ning on an ev-er spin-ning reel. As the im-ag-es un-

wind, Like the cir-cles that you find in the wind-mills of your mind!

YELLOW SUBMARINE
from YELLOW SUBMARINE

Words and Music by JOHN LENNON
and PAUL McCARTNEY

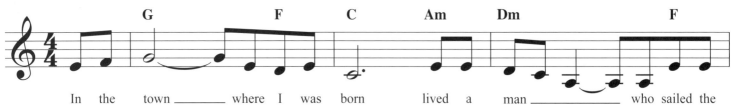

In the town _____ where I was born lived a man _____ who sailed the

sea. And he told _____ us of his life in the

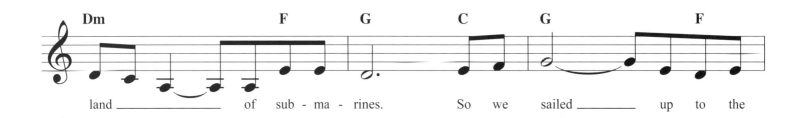

land _____ of sub-ma-rines. So we sailed _____ up to the

sun till we found _____ the sea of green. And we

lived _____ be-neath the waves in our yel-low sub-ma-rine.

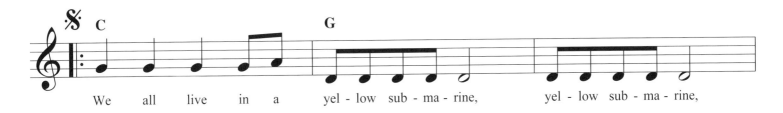

We all live in a yel - low sub - ma - rine, yel - low sub - ma - rine,

yel - low sub - ma - rine. We all live in a yel - low sub - ma - rine,

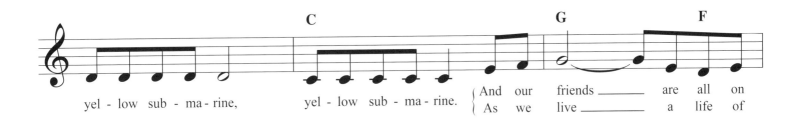

yel - low sub - ma - rine, yel - low sub - ma - rine.
{ And our friends _____ are all on
{ As we live _____ a life of

board, man - y more of them live next door. And the band _____ be - gins to
ease, ev - 'ry one of us has all we need. Sky of blue _____ and sea of

play: *(Instrumental)*

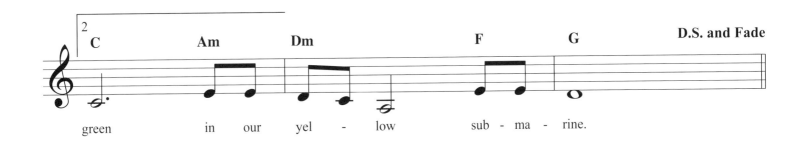

D.S. and Fade

green in our yel - low sub - ma - rine.

YOU LIGHT UP MY LIFE
from YOU LIGHT UP MY LIFE

Words and Music by
JOSEPH BROOKS

Moderately slow

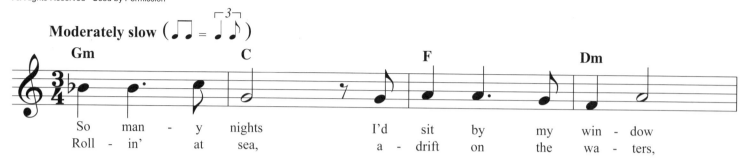

So man - y nights I'd sit by my win - dow
Roll - in' at sea, a - drift on the wa - ters,

wait - ing for some - one ___ to sing me his song.
could it be fi - n'lly ___ I'm turn - ing for home.

So man - y dreams I kept deep in - side me, a -
Fi - n'lly a chance to say, "Hey! I love you."

lone in the dark, but now you've come a - long.)
Nev - er a - gain to ___ be all a - lone.)
And

you light up my life. You give me

YOU'LL BE IN MY HEART*
(Pop Version)
from TARZAN™

Words and Music by
PHIL COLLINS

Moderately

Come, stop your cry-ing; it will be all right. __ Just take my hand,

hold it tight. ____ I will pro - tect you from all a - round __ you.

I will be here; don't you cry. For one so small you seem so strong. __
Why can't they un - der - stand the way we feel? __

My arms will hold you, keep you safe and warm. __ This bond be - tween us
They just don't trust __ what they can't ex - plain. __ I know we're dif - f'rent, but

can't be bro - ken. I will be here; don't you cry. 'Cause
deep in - side __ us we're not that dif - f'rent at all. And

you'll be in my heart, yes, you'll be in my heart from

* TARZAN® Owned by Edgar Rice Burroughs, Inc. and Used by Permission.
© Burroughs/Disney

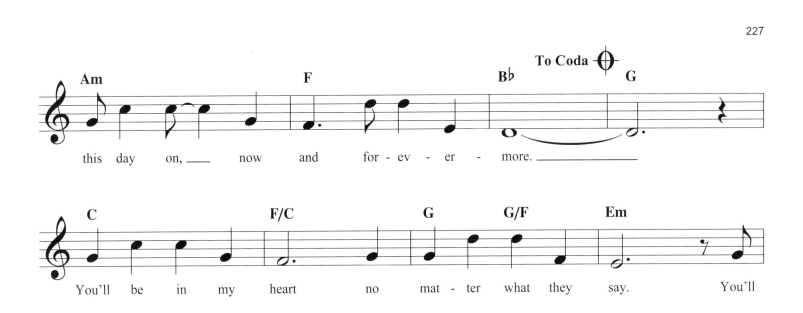

this day on, ___ now and for - ev - er - more. _____

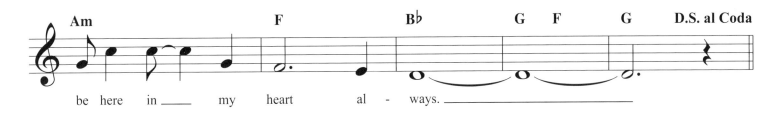

You'll be in my heart no mat - ter what they say. You'll

be here in ___ my heart al - ways. _____

Don't lis - ten to them, __ 'cause what do they know? __ We
des - ti - ny calls you, you must __ be strong. __ I

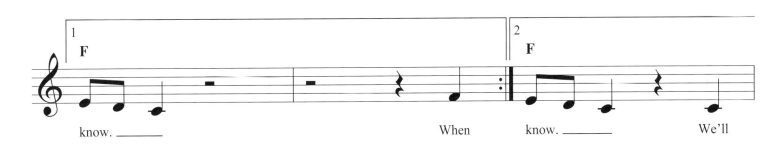

need each oth - er to have, to hold. __ } They'll see in time, I
may not be with you, but you've got to hold on. ___

know. _____ When know. _____ We'll

show them to - geth - er; 'cause you'll be in my heart. Be - lieve me, you'll be in my

CHORD SPELLER

C chords

C	C–E–G
Cm	C–E♭–G
C7	C–E–G–B♭
Cdim	C–E♭–G♭
C+	C–E–G♯

C♯ or D♭ chords

C♯	C♯–F–G♯
C♯m	C♯–E–G♯
C♯7	C♯–F–G♯–B
C♯dim	C♯–E–G
C♯+	C♯–F–A

D chords

D	D–F♯–A
Dm	D–F–A
D7	D–F♯–A–C
Ddim	D–F–A♭
D+	D–F♯–A♯

E♭ chords

E♭	E♭–G–B♭
E♭m	E♭–G♭–B♭
E♭7	E♭–G–B♭–D♭
E♭dim	E♭–G♭–A
E♭+	E♭–G–B

E chords

E	E–G♯–B
Em	E–G–B
E7	E–G♯–B–D
Edim	E–G–B♭
E+	E–G♯–C

F chords

F	F–A–C
Fm	F–A♭–C
F7	F–A–C–E♭
Fdim	F–A♭–B
F+	F–A–C♯

F♯ or G♭ chords

F♯	F♯–A♯–C♯
F♯m	F♯–A–C♯
F♯7	F♯–A♯–C♯–E
F♯dim	F♯–A–C
F♯+	F♯–A♯–D

G chords

G	G–B–D
Gm	G–B♭–D
G7	G–B–D–F
Gdim	G–B♭–D♭
G+	G–B–D♯

G♯ or A♭ chords

A♭	A♭–C–E♭
A♭m	A♭–B–E♭
A♭7	A♭–C–E♭–G♭
A♭dim	A♭–B–D
A♭+	A♭–C–E

A chords

A	A–C♯–E
Am	A–C–E
A7	A–C♯–E–G
Adim	A–C–E♭
A+	A–C♯–F

B♭ chords

B♭	B♭–D–F
B♭m	B♭–D♭–F
B♭7	B♭–D–F–A♭
B♭dim	B♭–D♭–E
B♭+	B♭–D–F♯

B chords

B	B–D♯–F♯
Bm	B–D–F♯
B7	B–D♯–F♯–A
Bdim	B–D–F
B+	B–D♯–G

Important Note: A slash chord (C/E, G/B) tells you that a certain bass note is to be played under a particular harmony. In the case of C/E, the chord is C and the bass note is E.

HAL LEONARD PRESENTS
FAKE BOOKS FOR BEGINNERS!

Entry-level fake books! These books feature larger-than-most fake book notation with simplified harmonies and melodies – and all songs are in the key of C. An introduction addresses basic instruction on playing from a fake book.

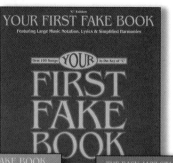

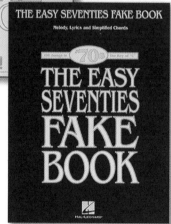

Your First Fake Book
00299529.............................$22.99

The Easy Fake Book
00240144.............................$19.99

The Simplified Fake Book
00299494.............................$22.99

The Beatles Easy Fake Book
00171200 ....$25.00

The Easy Broadway Fake Book
00276670.............................$19.99

The Easy Children's Fake Book
00240428 ....$19.99

The Easy Christian Fake Book
00240328.............................$19.99

The Easy Christmas Carols Fake Book
00238187 ....$19.99

The Easy Christmas Songs Fake Book
00277913.............................$19.99

The Easy Classic Rock Fake Book
00240389.............................$24.99

The Easy Classical Fake Book
00240262.............................$19.99

The Easy Country Fake Book
00240319.............................$22.99

The Easy Disney Fake Book
00275405.............................$24.99

The Easy Folksong Fake Book
00240360.............................$22.99

The Easy 4-Chord Fake Book
00118752 ....$19.99

The Easy G Major Fake Book
00142279 ....$19.99

The Easy Gospel Fake Book
00240169.............................$19.99

The Easy Hymn Fake Book
00240207.............................$19.99

The Easy Jazz Standards Fake Book
00102346.............................$19.99

The Easy Love Songs Fake Book
00159775 ....$24.99

The Easy Pop/Rock Fake Book
00141667 ....$24.99

The Easy 3-Chord Fake Book
00240388 ....$19.99

The Easy Worship Fake Book
00240265.............................$22.99

More of the Easy Worship Fake Book
00240362 ....$22.99

The Easy '20s Fake Book
00240336 ....$19.99

The Easy '30s Fake Book
00240335 ....$19.99

The Easy '40s Fake Book
00240252.............................$19.99

The Easy '50s Fake Book
00240255.............................$22.99

The Easy '60s Fake Book
00240253.............................$22.99

The Easy '70s Fake Book
00240256.............................$22.99

The Easy '80s Fake Book
00240340 ....$24.99

The Easy '90s Fake Book
00240341.............................$19.99

HAL•LEONARD®
halleonard.com

Prices, contents and availability subject to change without notice.

0421
128